W0091626

SAGE was founded in 1965 by Sara Miller McCune to support the dissemination of usable knowledge by publishing innovative and high-quality research and teaching content. Today, we publish over 900 journals, including those of more than 400 learned societies, more than 800 new books per year, and a growing range of library products including archives, data, case studies, reports, and video. SAGE remains majority-owned by our founder, and after Sara's lifetime will become owned by a charitable trust that secures our continued independence.

Los Angeles | London | New Delhi | Singapore | Washington DC | Melbourne

ADVANCE PRAISE

I have known Sidharth for many years now—first as his teacher at IIM Calcutta and second as a co-panellist on numerous interview panels. As a result, I have seen his career progress and his career graph rise, even as he has expanded his own horizons. He is that rare breed among managers—a reflective manager. Also, he has always had the ability to question his own assumptions. Both of these attributes are present in his new book where he draws upon the wealth of his own experience as well as that of others to provide an insightful analysis into strategy and strategic thinking from the standpoint of a practitioner. Along the way, he invites the reader to rethink what effective strategic thinking is all about.

Mritiunjoy Mohanty, *Senior Professor of Economics, IIM Calcutta*

Mr Sidharth Balakrishna has delivered management development programmes (MDPs) to several industry participants over the last few years including at New Delhi Institute of Management (NDIM) and always received stellar feedback. I am glad that he has now put down the approach and tools that he uses in this book to reach a wider audience who will benefit immensely from his emphasis on clarity of thought and structured approach in strategy and decision-making. The book is comprehensive in scope and has much for both seasoned industry executives and young professionals who seek to navigate through the corporate world. In particular, his approach towards strategy and innovation will help executives develop an 'intrapreneurial mindset' that can make a big difference to individuals and organizations.

Dr V. M. Bansal, *Chairman, NDIM*

I have known Sidharth Balakrishna for several years now while he has been leading strategy for major Indian corporate houses. His approach and willingness to pursue new avenues of thinking, as exemplified in his book, have helped him and the companies he has worked for immensely, and will surely likewise benefit the readers of this book.

Rooma Kumar Bussi, *Managing Director, Trade and Invest, British Columbia*

Mr Sidharth Balakrishna has been an adjunct faculty member at Great Lakes Institute of Management, Gurgaon, where he has received top-class feedback from students in terms of content, delivery and bison building. Students really enjoy his practical aspects that he brings to the sessions. In this book, he continues with his straightforward approach, stressing on simple yet highly effective ways towards strategy formulation and innovation. I know him as a voracious reader, thinker and practitioner. I am glad that he has shared his learnings from working with some of the major corporate houses in the country with a wider audience.

Dr Vikas Prakash Singh, *Director, PGDM Programme, Great Lakes Institute of Management*

Sidharth has emerged as a mentor and inspiration to many graduate and postgraduate students of Shri Ram College of Commerce (SRCC). His book and techniques will now inspire many to be more effective in their professions due to their lucidity and potential impact.

Dr Anil Kumar, *Head of Department and Course Coordinator, SRCC (GBO)*

Sidharth Balakrishna, with his unique multi-industry senior leadership experience and multidisciplinary approach, has written a very simple and de-jargonized book on how one can create a strategy that creates winners. The book focuses a lot on examples, solutions and ideas from the future. I would certainly say that it is a must-read for all MBA students and management practitioners, entrepreneurs, CEOs and anyone who runs a business. Reading this book will deliver ROI in more ways than one. The book, dare I say, could change your life and improve your business. It is a thought creator.

Dr Annurag Batra, *Chairman, BW Businessworld Group; Founder, Exchange4media*

Sidharth Balakrishna is one of those senior executives who also have a strong passion for teaching. His classes have received excellent feedback from the executive batches at Faculty of Management Studies (FMS), University of Delhi. In this book, he stresses on a structured and analytical approach towards strategy and decision-making, which will surely benefit readers. His approach towards changing one's mindset to achieve different results is indeed a very useful technique to drive innovation.

Sunita Singh Sengupta, *PhD, Head and Dean, FMS, University of Delhi*

I have known Sidharth for a number of years and was impressed by his structured approach towards strategy and problem-solving. He helped develop innovative and practical approaches to many difficult issues on the projects that we worked on together, and led the team to deliver results in challenging circumstances. I am glad he has encapsulated some of these techniques in this book, which no doubt will benefit readers across the spectrum. Indeed, such a book that stresses on combining both true strategic thinking with rigour and analysis of implementation from a practical standpoint was long overdue. The examples used in the book are a testimony to the author's ability to draw lessons from a wide variety of experiences and draw insightful inferences.

R. C. M. Reddy, *CEO, IL&FS Education and Technology Services*

Sidharth Balakrishna brings insights and advice that can change the discourse for start-ups. His first-hand experience in the corporate corridors makes it more trustworthy for the newcomers in business. What's needed is a simple and executable idea for start-ups and SB has loads of it.

Mehraj Dube, *Head of Marketing, ABP News*

I have always been impressed with Sidharth's analytical, problem-solving skills, and his approach towards strategy. I had an opportunity to work with him on several strategic projects at Essel Group to tackle complex business problems using innovation and build new efficient business models. It was an enriching experience to learn from his skills. The book is a great representation of his insights and best practices. It's a great read for anyone looking to learn new-age, implementable methods of business strategy and innovation.

Rohan Tyagi, *Marketing Head India, M&E, TikTok*

CUT
to the
CHASE

CUT
to the
CHASE

A No-Nonsense Approach towards
Strategy and Problem-Solving

Sidharth Balakrishna

Los Angeles | London | New Delhi
Singapore | Washington DC | Melbourne

First published in 2020 by

SAGE Publications India Pvt Ltd
B1/I-1 Mohan Cooperative Industrial Area
Mathura Road, New Delhi 110 044, India
www.sagepub.in

SAGE Publications Inc
2455 Teller Road
Thousand Oaks, California 91320, USA

SAGE Publications Ltd
1 Oliver's Yard, 55 City Road
London EC1Y 1SP, United Kingdom

SAGE Publications Asia-Pacific Pte Ltd
18 Cross Street #10-10/11/12
China Square Central
Singapore 048423

Published by Vivek Mehra for SAGE Publications India Pvt Ltd. Typeset in 11/14.5 pt Sabon by Fidus Design Pvt. Ltd, Chandigarh.

Library of Congress Cataloging-in-Publication Data Available

ISBN: 978-93-5388-270-9 (PB)

SAGE Team: Manisha Mathews, Ankit Verma and Kanika Mathur

Dedicated to

Shreshth (Bidu)

Thank you for choosing a SAGE product!
If you have any comment, observation or feedback,
I would like to personally hear from you.

Please write to me at **contactceo@sagepub.in**

Vivek Mehra, Managing Director and CEO, SAGE India.

CONTENTS

FOREWORD

Sometimes, you read a book and it fills you with this weird evangelical zeal, and you become convinced that the shattered world will never be put back together unless and until all living humans read the book.

—John Green, *The Fault in Our Stars*

There are many books on strategy I have read and followed, but this is one book which evokes such a feeling.

We live in a truly VUCA world—it is volatile, uncertain, complex and ambiguous—and a very fast-changing business scenario where businesses are being morphed and annihilated and new entrants out of nowhere are creating new empires.

In such a fast-changing world, how does one strategize and stay relevant and thrive? Sidharth Balakrishna, with his unique multi-industry senior leadership experience and multidisciplinary approach, has written a very simple, de-jargonized, anecdotal and funny account of how the world is changing and how one can create a strategy that creates winners. The simplicity and practicality of the book is its USP. It focuses a lot on examples, solutions and ideas from the future. He has used plenty of examples from the Indian and international contexts, for example, Nano and why it failed and what are the lessons from it .The book is relatable and practical. It is not a book from an armchair strategist.

The book lives up to what Michael Porter said: 'Strategy is about making choices, trade-offs; it's about deliberately choosing to be different.' It tells you how to create differentiation and purpose and weave it as part of the strategy.

'Hope is not a strategy,' said Vince Lombardi. The book gives you not only hope but also a practical toolkit and thinking process for framing strategy and then implementing it. Strategy at one time was thought of as very complex and bastion of management; in reality, it is about purpose and being responsive to environment. This is what this book elucidates. If I had to rename Sidharth's book, I would call it 'Strategy That Makes Sense'.

The book is a labour of love and an experiential journey. I have read the book and look forward to re-reading it as well!

I would certainly say that it is a must-read for all MBA students and management practitioners, entrepreneurs, CEOs and anyone who runs a business.

Speakers at conferences can do well to quote from the book and make the audiences smile with the anecdotal examples in it.

I would like to end by saying that while reading this, you do not ever feel that you are reading a strategy book which sometimes can be boring and too theoretical. This is a fun and interesting read, which you can revisit whenever you wish. That is the strength of this book.

Reading it will deliver ROI in more ways than one. This book, dare I say, could change your life and improve your business. It is a thought creator.

Dr Annurag Batra
Author; entrepreneur; TV show host; angel investor;
media mogul and an eternal optimist;
Founder, Exchange4media; Chairman,
BW Businessworld Group

PREFACE

There have been many inspirations for writing this book, particularly those who suggested I write another one given the relative success of my earlier books and that it had been some time since I wrote another one!

I am grateful to the team at SAGE who approached me quite a few months ago asking me to consider penning down a few thoughts on strategy and management. While I was too tied up with work to address the suggestion at that time, I gradually found the opportunity and time to get down to writing this book.

I have intended to focus on the practical aspects of strategy and management, rather than lay too much emphasis on theory and thus have included as many real-life examples and anecdotes as possible. They all closely resemble my experiences. Moreover, I apologize if I end up hurting anyone's feelings through anything in this book.

Real-life experiences have given me much food for thought and rumination. I have had the fortune of having worked directly with many well-known companies, both in industry directly or in my consulting roles. I have always taken time to ponder over things and seek clarity in thought and action; and that has provided the basis for my understanding and treatment of issues pertaining to strategy and problem-solving in this book.

I consider it fortunate that throughout the ups and downs of my career, I feel that I have been able to approach all tasks with enthusiasm, pausing to reflect often on what has worked and what hasn't, which has culminated in my penning these thoughts. I have also been fortunate to have access to senior management in most of the companies where I have worked, learning a lot from them and how they have looked at business challenges. Eventually, I found myself in that role myself and put many of my learnings to hopefully good use!

I have also had the occasion to share my learnings by being part of the faculty at several training programmes and Management Development Programmes (MDPs) in India and abroad, and the feedback I have received has helped me sharpen some of my thoughts.

I hope you will enjoy reading this book and look forward to your valuable feedback. I can be reached at sidharth.balakrishna@gmail.com.

ACKNOWLEDGEMENTS

I would like to thank the following people: Dr Subhas Chandra for giving me the opportunity to work in the media space and provide me with a leadership role in his group; Nilesh Jain, P. Elango, Sundeep Bhandari and S. V. Nair at Cairn India for their guidance in my career; of course, my wife, for her contribution to some aspects and one particular chapter in this book; and my friends and colleagues at IIM Indore, FMS, SRCC, NDIM, IQPC and other organizations that have given me the opportunity to teach many of the concepts mentioned in this book.

I also thank the senior professionals who have contributed stories of their journey towards this book and helped me with their guidance and testimonials.

Finally, I am grateful to the team at SAGE, particularly Ms Manisha whose thoughtful comments certainly provided for better content in this book.

Chapter 1

Oil Is Found between the Ears

If you always do what you always did, you will always get what you always got.
—Albert Einstein

Minds are like parachutes; they work best when open.
—Thomas Dewar

It was a cold winter day in Delhi; foggy outside, but cosy and comfortable in the offices of the oil and gas company where I was working. I had just come in though and it had been so cold outside that my fingers were still a little numb and prevented me from using the keyboard of my laptop properly.

I had nothing better to do on that particular day, so I decided to grab a cup of coffee and try to use the time for 'personal growth' as my company used to put it. I went to the common IT repository of old documents and presentations, trying to find something that would catch my attention.

One PowerPoint file caught my attention due to its catchy title. I opened the file and glanced at the first picture. Immediately, a sudden feeling of warmth came over me, pushing out the winter cold. I spent a long time looking at the slide, taking in its message, and the more I looked at it, the more it appealed to me.

Glance over this picture that I had first seen well over seven years ago. It still draws me to ponder over it and many, who have attended my corporate presentations or even students who have seen the presentations I have made at their institutes, will recall that I often opened my presentations with this slide.

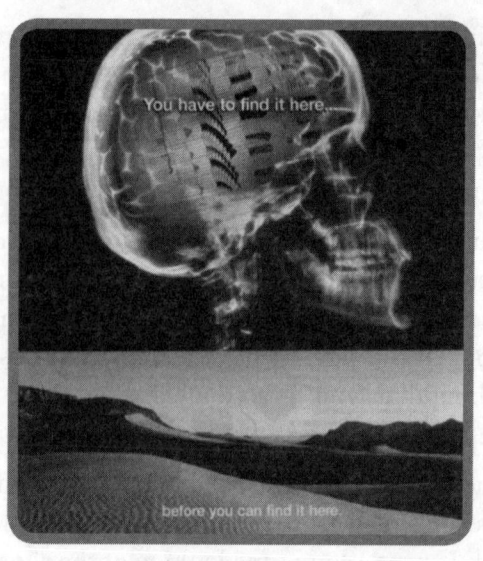

We are paid to think and be innovative!

Stop creativity and you stop progress!

The top panel of the slide, the one with the picture of a human skull or brain, has a few words. It says, 'You have to find it here.' The panel below shows a desert, with the simple words: 'Before you can find it here'.

I have asked many people to give their views on this slide and have received several insightful answers and thoughts when I have guided them to interpret it. Many have seen and have been inspired by the simple message that the slide wishes to convey. A few have even come up to me years after I first showed them the picture and told me how deep an impression it had made on them.

What do the two pictures and the accompanying words wish to convey?

The immediate description of the slide is about finding oil, with the top panel depicting the human brain, hence, in a manner speaking of or representing human ingenuity.

How does one find oil? One has to drill to find this precious resource. So valuable is the resource and so widespread is its use in transport and in the making of petrochemicals and fuels, that some analysts have called the age we live in as the 'age of the hydrocarbon man'.

But how does one decide where to drill? One has to first conduct seismic surveys (and other kinds of surveys). What do these surveys give you?

The quick answer is that they give you plenty of data and information, in fact, literally gigabytes and terabytes of data. But all this is relatively easy! The crux of the matter lies elsewhere.

Some of the world's best and the ones with the most specialized knowledge—the seismic analysts, the reservoir engineers, the geologists, geophysicists, and so on—are required to analyse or interpret the seismic data obtained. Each of them comes up with different thoughts and interpretations; sometimes they agree, sometimes they don't.

Dr John Doran, the founder of Command Petroleum, a small oil company, which was to have a major impact as far as India was concerned, is said to have believed that 'the best oil reservoir in the world is to be found between the ears'. 'While oil and gas fields are physically located in the ground, they are actually found and developed in the minds of men and women.'

Although I cannot be sure, perhaps on that day, I had stumbled on one of the slides that Dr Doran himself had used. In any case, I had certainly stumbled upon his philosophy, that is, as far as his thoughts relating to the discovery of hydrocarbon resources were concerned.

There are however, many thoughts which come to mind on studying these pictures.

The bottom panel depicting finding of oil, represents the action to be taken. Before the action, there is so much that needs to be worked on in the mind. Indeed, what we do in the mind actually determines the success or failure of the action.

The story of Cairn's discovery of the Mangala oil field, India's largest onshore field and the second largest oil discovery ever in the country (after Mumbai High by ONGC) represents this fact. Multinational oil companies like Shell (and even ONGC) had explored the acreage near Barmer in Rajasthan without making any significant discovery.

Shell sold the rights of the field to a then obscure Scottish firm called Cairn, which in turn, drilled as many as a dozen dry wells (no discovery) before suddenly hitting gold and finding the field now called 'Mangala' (or 'auspicious'). I was recounting this story in Muscat, Oman, a few years ago, at a conference held at the beautiful coastal resort BarrAl Jissah, and a senior Shell executive said she agreed with me, pointing out that it took a lot of courage to go and drill after the early failures in an area where even the seismic data was not looking all that promising.

Courage, indeed, was demonstrated aplenty by the small Scottish firm and its employees. Cairn gradually rose to become India's second largest oil producer (after the National Oil Company, ONGC) and the operator of India's largest onshore field at Barmer in Rajasthan. Although I was not part of the initial journey, joining in 2010 soon after actual commercial oil production started (in 2009), I often thought of the challenges involved in producing oil and building world-class oil infrastructure in such a remote part of the country.

Barmer, even today, appears to the first-time visitor as a godforsaken town beyond the desert landscape; its relatively low population density adds to the feeling of emptiness. How it must have been then in the late 1990s and early 2000s when prospecting was going on?

Let us keep in mind that finding oil was only the first part of the adventure. Building an infrastructure, including safety aspects, as expected from the oil and gas industry which deals with a highly hazardous substance, was an even bigger challenge.

The biggest issue came when it was realized that the crude from the Rajasthan fields was 'waxy'; it resembled shoe polish at normal room temperature and did not flow in conventional pipelines. Cairn had to construct the world's longest pipeline, which had to be heated continuously, to ferry the oil to the Gujarat refineries. Such a technology of continuously heating the pipeline had never before been implemented in the country (and hasn't been replicated since).

How did such a small company build this kind of an infrastructure, including the laying out of the world's longest pipeline? How did it manage to get the contractors, including the local ones, and adhere to safety standards that were best-in-class?

While to explain this would entail many chapters, it would suffice to say here that this needed a lot of courage, belief, meticulous planning, problem-solving and innovation.

Chronology of a Success Story: How a Small Scottish Firm Grew to Become India's Second Largest Oil Producer

1995: Royal Dutch Shell signs a pact with Centre to explore and operate RJ-ON-90/1 oil block in Barmer. Cairn Energy owns 10 per cent in the lease.

1998: Cairn acquires 27 per cent of the project.

2002: Cairn takes 100 per cent control of the project with Shell selling its stake for a pittance.

2004: 3.7 billion barrels of oil equivalent (boe) found in Barmer's Mangala oilfield, India's biggest onshore hydrocarbon find in two decades.

2005: ONGC buys 30 per cent in the Cairn project.

2009: Production begins at Mangala. A pipeline is constructed to ship output to Gujarat's Salaya port.

2012: Bhagyam oilfield, the second largest in Barmer, starts production.

2013: Aishwariya, the third largest field becomes operational.

Let us draw an analogy from the game of cricket, which so popular amongst us. When the two captains walk out to the toss, each has more or less the same information—on weather, playing conditions, pitch conditions, and so on, but while one captain wishes to bat first if he wins the toss, the other prefers to bowl. Both reach opposing conclusions after processing the same base data.

Real life is not as black or white as having to choose to bat or bowl first. In reality, we are faced with a continuum of possible choices and huge volumes of data and information owing to search engines and data sources such as Google and a myriad other resources.

The complexity we are faced with today is the ability to sieve through all that information and make decisions, and the right ones. Truly, one is 'paid to think' as the words below the picture on page 4 indicate. This is what separates the good corporate executive from the average one: quality of one's decision-making skills and ability to sieve through all the information and decide what to do are essential characteristics.

Consulting companies, such as McKinsey, BCG, Bain and so on understand this well. In their interview process applicants are asked to read what are called 'Case Studies' and decide on a course of action. A case study provides the outline of a situation, with some issues that need to be addressed. All the relevant information and data is provided in the case, hence, the applicant's prior knowledge does not matter. What matters clearly is that having looked at the same set of data and information points, how a successful applicant is able to explain his course of action logically and lucidly.

Where should one set up a new manufacturing plant—in China, Vietnam or India? If within India, would it be in Tamil Nadu, Gujarat or Andhra Pradesh? And within Gujarat, would it be near Ahmedabad or Surat? So, the choices for a modern-day executive in a globalized world are endless, and so is the data and information that he or she has or can obtain quickly.

Here what is most crucial is to take the right decision. And, where is it to be done? In one's mind, between the ears.

ALL IN THE MIND

Having taken a decision, however easy or difficult it might have been, marks only the beginning. The example of Cairn, as well as the cricket analogy indicates that apart from decision-making, there is still a lot to be done, and that too in the mind. The mind is where:

- the vision is conceived and where it resides to inspire
- planning towards the execution—of that vision—is to be done
- new ideas must come if things do not always go well
- possibilities and trends to understand realities must be analysed
- problems must be understood and solved
- beliefs and assumptions, which sometimes lead to spectacular success or catastrophic failure, lie.
- stories that inspire and motivate are born
- innovation, creativity and new ways of looking at things begin
- priorities are decided. This is perhaps the most crucial skill of all. Things are not good or bad in the corporate sector, they need to be prioritized—who should be served first? Where to allocate any spare resource? What comes first and what is next? Who is first in line for a promotion and who is second?
- one decides to be bold or do things in conventional ways

The mind is also where, at times, ideals give way to despondency or cynicism.

In this book, we shall examine some of these aspects in detail and understand how we can get better at getting ideas, innovating, planning, strategizing, solving problems, being creative, avoiding disabling biases or assumptions and the like.

A crucial skill, therefore, for an executive, today, at any level, is the ability to analyse (in other words, 'analytical ability'). This book provides some aspects and examples of how executives can hone these abilities so as to make better decisions and avoid common pitfalls.

I would rate this ability to analyse well, along with problem-solving skills—the ability to drill down (being analytical) and find the underlying cause or issue and fix the problem—as the two most important skills that any corporate executive should have; hence, the two most important abilities students in any management school should seek to learn.

The United Nations understands the power of the mind as well as any of us. The preamble to the constitution of the United Nations Educational, Scientific and Cultural Organisation (UNESCO) says, 'That since wars begin in the minds of men, it is in the minds of men that the defences of peace must be constructed....'

It was certainly one man's warped thinking that led the world into what came to be called 'the Second World War'. Think then, that if the mind's energies and capabilities were to be properly harnessed, how could we all benefit?

On a slightly different note, these human skills—analysis and problem-solving—will have an ever-increasing relevance in a world where Artificial Intelligence (AI) will soon play a game-changing role. Most tasks that are of a repetitive (or 'mechanical') nature will be executed by software programs and algorithms.

On the other hand, human beings who have an ability to analyse and provide the 'why' behind 'what happened', understand the underlying causes, sentiments and emotion; and use these to evaluate possibilities of what might happen in future, continue to be in demand and earn a disproportionately higher pay. Workers who merely perform tasks that do not involve thinking and analysis, however, will be most at risk of losing their jobs to AI algorithms.

An example of this is what has come to be called 'robo journalism'. The Associated Press (AP), one of the world's largest news agencies, has assigned the task of writing up quarterly-earnings news to an algorithm. Refer to the article below called 'Would you know this story was written by a robot?' and try and judge who has authored the story!

The system uses natural language processing to synthesize information from a variety of sources, and the articles are widely circulated by outlets like Yahoo Finance, *Huffington Post* and *Investor's Business Daily*. *Washington Post*, on similar lines, a few years ago, came up with a 'robo-journalist', christened as 'Heliograf', who produced a number of factual reports on sports events.

The AP has used the technology extensively to expand the number of companies it covers—from around 400 per quarter to more than 4,000—leading to many benefits, including increasing the depth and breadth of the stock market. As reports were produced on a greater number of companies, more people felt they knew enough about them to actively trade their shares.

But look closely at an article written by an algorithm, such as the one here. The story was written entirely by a bot. But you will notice a crucial aspect: the story here has only facts, plenty of them indeed, but no analysis. The company in question has seen its quarterly earnings decline and miss expectations but there is no analysis as to why this happened; nor any analysis of what might occur in future as a consequence of these numbers. The report states the facts and only the facts!

Human beings, hence, are needed to supplement this information with quality analysis; such an example illustrates how bots and humans can work together to enhance value. The computer program can generate a fact-based story much faster than a human reporter, thus helping the media agency beat others in getting their story to the market. Quality human editors can then add their views, analysis and predictions to provide more knowledge to the reader.

But the bottom line is clear. Those jobs that require thinking or creative skills will need humans; those requiring mechanical conduct of repetitive tasks where much thought is not involved will see major disruptions.

The future, therefore, will belong to those who use their minds and intellect to take decisions, solve problems and analyse issues. I strongly feel that the skills that will be most in demand are analytical thinking and problem-solving, while routine and mundane tasks of information gathering and processing will be left to software programs and bots.

It will therefore be crucial for all of us to ensure that our intellect and ability to analyse (or make 'sense' of what is happening and why) is well developed. This means asking oneself and understanding 'the why' behind every issue and understanding the consequences of actions and decisions both in the short and long run. It will all be in the mind!

Training the Mind to take Better Decisions

The mind has to be trained to make decisions—this will be a key skill for executives in all companies to have going forward. Executives will gradually be paid to solve problems and take decisions, and not just provide information; the latter being a task that search engines and AI will do much better than humans.

So how can you take better decisions?

I strongly suggest that executives work on their *approach* while having to take any sort of decision. Some common decisions could be:

- Where should your company invest—in which location? India or China, Vietnam or the Philippines? Within India, where? Mumbai, Gujarat or Tamil Nadu?

- Which product does one focus on if your company has a portfolio of products?

- Which customer segment to focus on?

To arrive at an optimal decision, I suggest the following approach:

First, identify the parameters important to the company at that time. The parameters would depend on the nature of product the company makes or the service it provides, or the location in which it operates. Let us take an example here.

Assume your firm assembles electronics, putting together several components, and exports the finished product to several countries. What parameters are important for such a company?

Clearly, if one is assembling products comprising many components and then exporting them, there are at least two very important considerations:

- The import and export duties on the components being procured and the finished product, respectively.

- Supply chain efficiencies so that there is quick turnaround and stock is not held up.

In addition, tax rates are usually a major consideration.

Now, we can take another example. Let us suppose you are a steel producer. In this case, the important parameters would be:

- Access to raw materials used to make steel and their costs such as iron ore and limestone.

- Logistics to move these raw materials to your manufacturing location and the finished steel to your customers.

- Power costs, as making steel requires a lot of power.

(As an aside, where do you think India scores on these parameters? Do you feel these important parameters support the 'Make in India' initiative?)

In my experience, often disagreements, even at the level of the board of directors, are due to the fact that different people are considering different parameters. So first, get this right—identify the parameters crucial in respect of the decision that is to be made. Do not make a laundry list of parameters; however, focus on the top three or maximum five parameters.

Being able to identify and narrow down what is crucial to your business is a key management skill. I have seen too many senior managers asking their team to collect 'all possible information' when a decision is being made. This is a wrong approach. Asking for 'all possible information' makes your team run around like headless chickens, not knowing exactly what they seek.

Further, such an approach only wastes time. Even if your team was to get a lot of rich information, it will create an issue, for all the data rarely points to the same direction. There are always some positives and some negatives that will be found, given all the data that has been gathered, and hence you may end up suffering from 'analysis paralysis'.

Therefore, being a good manager with good 'decision-making skills' entails deciding what to examine in greater detail because it is important and what is less so can be left out. This must, of course, be done in an unbiased manner.

Second, decide the relative importance of these parameters, in a manner of speaking, you have to assign them weightages with the relative weights reflecting their relative importance.

For example, are tax rates the most important consideration or something else? Costs of raw materials or the cost of power?

Again, this calls for good 'managerial skills'. Now, you are not only deciding what is important, but what is more important than something else. Everything cannot be equally important.

The third step is now to collect information about these parameters. For example, what are the import and export duties in the countries being considered as a potential location for your company's new manufacturing location? What are the power costs and the tax rates? What is the cost and distance of sources of raw material?

This is a structured approach towards decision-making. The structure avoids biases creeping into your process, demands that you consider trade-offs and identify crucial variables, thus avoiding knee-jerk reactions.

Finally, after going through this structured approach, you are now in a position to take a decision.

BUT, stop here for a moment. Before, you finalize your decision, take a look at BOTH of the following:

- The short-term benefits and consequences of your decision.
- The long-term consequences.

This involves a closer study of what is often clubbed together as 'risks'. This also needs close scrutiny. Most importantly, something that makes sense in the short term like a 'special set of favourable circumstances' may not make sense in the long run.

For example, diversifying into a new sector because there are licences or raw material sources that are relatively cheap or some time-bound government scheme may NOT make sense in respect of a long-term view. A number of Indian companies realized this to their chagrin, when their diversifications into the power sector or even telecom turned sour, and in some cases, sunk the whole group for these were capital-intensive projects requiring large debts.

I know of one Indian promoter who started a new business because the asset required to run that business was available for acquisition at a dirt-cheap price. But the company soon realized that the cost to keep that asset going and well maintained was many more times the initial cost of the asset.

The bottom line is that short- and long-term considerations are attached to any decision. Consider both carefully before deciding that is the final step.

Chapter 2

The Man with the Cow

Nothing astonishes men so much as common sense and
plain dealing.
—Ralph Waldo Emerson

He that is down need fear no fall;
He that is low, no pride;
He that is humble ever shall
Have God to be his guide.
—John Bunyan

Have a close look at the picture below. This is one of my favourite pictures that I often show towards the end of any of my lectures on strategy and problem-solving.

Take some time and look at the picture closely. What do you see and how do you interpret this picture? Hint: there is no religious connotation to the picture.

Now think carefully about what the man in the picture has succeeded in doing. Spend some time on this and make mental notes of the various thoughts that come into your mind.

LOOK HONEY, NO FIXED COSTS

Let me bring a few management-related thoughts into this. There are two aspects at which every company is aiming. First, operate a company with an asset-light model. Tom Goodwin, an executive at the French media group Havas, is reportedly the first who pointed out:

- The world's largest taxi firm, Uber, owns no cars.
- The world's most popular media company, Facebook, creates no content.
- The world's most valuable retailer, Alibaba, carries no inventory.
- The world's largest accommodation provider, Airbnb, owns no property.

Looked at slightly differently, all companies, in recent times, are looking to increase their Return on Assets (ROA) or Return on Capital Employed (ROCE) or Return on Invested Capital (ROIC) and indeed, this is one of the metrics that an analyst should look at while tracking a company's performance for these metrics indicate how well a company is able to use the funds it obtains from shareholders and investors.

All strategy experts or management consultancies look to advise a company on improving these metrics so that they become more attractive to shareholders.

Second, and this is related to the first, every modern manager, especially those from the finance domain, seeks to change fixed costs into variable ones. Put in other words, convert costs that are not a function of output or business cycles to costs that do reflect changes in output and production.

Why is this so crucial in present times? One of the major reasons is that while business cycles and product lifecycles have shortened, customer preferences seem to be changing more rapidly. If one cannot get to a stage where one has no fixed assets (like AirBnB or Alibaba in the examples cited above), then in a world where risk and uncertainty is only increasing, one must certainly look to minimize inventory.

Large investments in plant and machinery in a world of ever-increasing change is no longer considered a great idea. Think of what would happen to the automobile firms who have invested millions, even billions of dollars, on factors that produce vehicles relying on the internal combustion engine, if the world was to suddenly shift to using electric vehicles or governments across the world decided to push through this change? They would see massive erosion of wealth with the metrics such as ROA, ROIC, and so on being turned on their heads very quickly.

Hence, there is preference towards making fixed costs variable and operating on an asset-light basis; companies who operate on such a model, at least theoretically, are more nimble and capable of responding to change.

The wave of outsourcing, which played itself out over the last decade, is much in line with this broad need. Outsourcing is indeed one of the best ways to convert fixed costs into a variable one and making the metrics look better, for example, by taking employees off the company's rolls and hiring skills as and when needed and in just the required numbers. By opting for contractual models and temporary staff, hiring temporary office space or using hot-seating arrangements companies can reduce fixed costs.

Now, take a look at the picture again. Using the points just mentioned, try to interpret this picture once more and note/ write down your thoughts.

COST CENTRE OR PROFIT CENTRE?

This is a picture I often use when asked to speak at various strategy sessions. Having taken the audience through my thoughts (as outlined in the earlier paragraphs), I tell my audience that the person in the photograph has done what most strategy consultants and advisors have not been able to ever do. How so? Let me explain.

First, think of the man as a company. What does the cow represent for the man? The answer is simple—it is an asset. How does the asset help him? The asset is of great importance to him—the cow provides milk which the man can sell and earn revenue.

Just like any asset, is there a cost associated with the asset?

There is, of course. The production of milk is directly related to how the man maintains the cow, particularly how well the cow is fed. As in any company, a profit is only earned as long as the revenues exceed the costs.

Therefore, in the context of the discussion, the man needs to maximize his profit by either increasing revenues or reducing costs.

Here is where this simple man, with certainly no technical or management background, has done so much better than Indian Institute of Technology (IIT) or Indian Institute of Management (IIM)-educated folks, including those who may have worked with the world's best firms. The cow is a 'revenue centre for the man'; while feeding the cow represents a 'cost centre'. What has the man done?

By taking the cow and standing in front of a temple, the man is able to get people who visit the temple to give him money to feed his cow.

Think of this! People are giving him money so that he can feed his own cow!

But more importantly, what has he achieved? Wonder of wonders, he has converted his cost centre (that of feeding the cow) into another revenue (hence, profit) source, just by using a bit of clever thinking!

The story is a simple one, but the conclusions one draws from it are important.

First, and most important, I use the story to tell my audience to be humble. The man in the picture, to reiterate, has had little formal education, but has succeeded in thinking of and doing what those of a more privileged background with much better education, may have struggled to do.

It is, therefore, of utmost importance to realize that while everyone may not have a great idea, one must always remember that a great idea can come from anywhere. Ideas and strategies are not the prerogative of the privileged few. Those who look for creative problem-solving, good strategy formulation and innovation, must keep their eyes open, talk to and learn from everyone amongst themselves.

Let us look at a practical example of converting a 'cost centre' into a 'profit centre'. I had the fortune of working with one of India's largest media houses for some time. For all media companies, the costs of 'content', that is, the cost of producing entertainment shows or news stories is significant; and in some cases, even more than the revenues that subscriptions (through consumers paying for watching the content) and advertising can bring back. Hence, most media companies struggle to manage these content costs.

But now, consider Facebook or YouTube. They 'source' the content from millions or even billions of people across the world. The content cost for these companies is virtually nil. Further, as viewers across the world watch the videos uploaded by millions or others on Facebook or YouTube, these companies are actually monetizing the content by inserting advertisements within the videos, even though they have not created the content! The cost centre for others (of creating content) has become a source of profit for these companies.

Look for such opportunities in your industry. Can a change in your business model turn the industry on its head? Can you do what the man with the cow has done?

IDEAS CAN COME FROM ANYWHERE!

I remember a story from the days when I was with Hindustan Unilever Ltd (HUL). It was my first job after I studied management at IIM Calcutta. I later learnt that it was perhaps first narrated by Mukul Deoras, who was then with HUL, and today, is a senior executive with Colgate Palmolive.

> A young Area Sales Manager (ASM) with HUL, was talking to one of his wholesalers on a hot, summer afternoon. Most HUL distributors, and indeed, distributors and wholesalers in general operated on a very small margin. The ASM noticed on the day that the owner of the wholesale establishment was away and in his absence, his son had taken charge of his father's establishment. The boy could not have been more than 16 or 17 years.
>
> The ASM was fresh out of a premier institute (like me at the time), and got chatting with the boy. Full of his newly learnt management theories, he soon started giving the younger boy some advice, and ended up by saying that his father shouldn't sell products on such a thin margin as it was never going to be sustainable.

The young 16-year-old smiled back. He quietly said to the ASM, 'No, you don't get it. We actually make a good amount of money on HUL products. We hold a couple of weeks of stock of HUL products. We get a seven-day credit from the distributor. Hence, in a manner of speaking, our investment is one week's stock....

'We turn over this stock almost 50 times a year. Hence, even with a 1 percent margin on each rotation of stock, our ROI comes to 50 percent.'

The ASM felt as if he had been punched. All that he had learnt during his MBA went out of the window. He realized that so much could be earned by rotating money—not just by margins on every transaction.

Clearly then, one must keep one's eyes, ears and mind open. You never know who can teach you a valuable lesson.

You must always keep in mind when you look around and talk to people that while doing so, you have to 'leave your crown in the shed'—you should not be the boss. Avoid pointing fingers, suggesting on-spot changes and looking for people or processes to blame. You are not to judge and review results. You need to collaborate with the team and find solutions to problems together.

As an illustration of this, I would like to share another personal anecdote. The conglomerate that I was working for had just started operating a cruise liner, one of the first in India, and I was looking for the kind of experiences that one could provide to customers while on the voyage to delight them. Most senior executives and experts from the sector spoke about the usual aspects that customers liked, namely, fine dining, entertainment options, including on-board movie screenings, games and fun events, and so on.

However, one person from the Human Resources Department, who had nothing whatsoever to do with this line of business, in a one-on-one discussion with me, outlined a really mind-blowing idea. He spoke about his friend who runs a tour company specializing in arranging tours to Rajasthan, in India, and providing extremely personalized experiences to his clientele, comprising mostly foreigners.

The tour-de-force of this tour company lies actually in the denouement: the tour ends with the traditional Rajasthani puppet show or 'katputli'. But the theme of the puppet show does not revolve around a traditional folk lore based on a Rajasthani hero or heroine, instead, the puppets enact scenes which the tour participants have personally experienced over the past few days with the tour manager. The puppet show is the story of the tour participants themselves!

The entire tour group is generally blown over and showers money on the puppeteers.

BACK TO THE UPANISHADS

What I have tried to outline in this chapter is perhaps nothing new—that age-old Indian wisdom has always emphasized the need to listen to, hear and learn from people of all walks of life, and that common sense is more important than mere knowledge.

The Upanishads and other books containing tales of wisdom often speak of how the most learned brahmins were bested in debates with the simple folk. A well-known story about Adi Shankaracharya is narrated:

One summer noon at Varanasi, Sri Shankara after taking a bath in the holy Ganga, was proceeding towards the temple of Lord Viswanath along with his disciples. He suddenly saw a person from a lower caste, coming along with his dogs in his way. He asked him to move away from his path.

However, the innocent man responded by asking the revered saint, 'Who are you asking to move aside, Sir? Are you demanding the self, or the body, to do so? If you are asking the physical body to move aside, you know that body is inert matter, how can it move aside at all? Also, in what respect is your body distinct and different from any other body? You say that you are firmly established and rooted in the Supreme Truth and there is but One non-dual entity—"One, without a second!" I see that your claim is all false! Is there any difference between a chandala and a brahmin from the viewpoint of the knower of the Truth? Is the sun's reflection on the water of the River Ganga different from that on the water of a drain or that in a glass of wine? Will the reflected sky be inferior in an earthen pot, compared to the one in a golden vessel?'

These insightful questions made the sage completely change his outlook and compose a famous poem entitled *Maneeshaa Panchakam* ('Maneeshaa' means conviction and 'Panchakam' denotes a collection of five. Sri Shankara, in this short composition of five verses, is considered to have brought out the essence of Vedanta with conviction). This story concerning Adi Shankara is often cited as an example as to how the greatest of scholars met his match in a person who was far less erudite and scholarly than him. The simple chandala, in this case, was able to make the sage realize that he too possessed an understanding of complex matters and could put across his innate wisdom in simple terms.

It is a testimony to the greatness of Adi Shankara that the great scholar was able to see beyond the chandala's outward appearance and pay attention to the truth he spoke. This aspect—to 'listen' to a person—is significant. It means to suspend judgement and evaluation and concentrate on the substance of what the other person is saying.

This is not done easily. Often, when someone speaks to us, we first 'assess him' as Adi Shankara started in the beginning of the story. He noticed the person's outward appearance and attributes such as his caste, and concluded the 'worth' of the person, believing that he would lack in spiritual attributes.

The story goes on to teach us not to jump to conclusions. One must not judge a book by its cover. The chandala was capable of thinking of complex human and spiritual matters like any brahmin or learned man! He too had something to offer, and deserved being listened to.

This aspect of genuinely listening to others was brought out to me in a performance review by one of my managers whom I truly admire. His name is Nilesh Jain. Despite having been educated in premier institutes—first engineering at IIT, Delhi, and then management from IIM Ahmedabad and then economics from the Chicago University where he was a gold medallist—Nilesh was one of the only people I know who genuinely demonstrated respect for other people's views, notwithstanding how foolish they sounded at times. While I often showed impatience with such beliefs and notions (and still do), Nilesh made many efforts at the time to get me to demonstrate genuine listening abilities.

He once narrated a story to me which spoke about three people travelling together on a train. Each of them ask the others about themselves. However, there is a big difference in the way they ask. The first person asks mechanically; though he is polite, he shows no real interest in the answers.

The second is merely curious as he has an ulterior motive—he wishes to show them how much better he has done as compared to them or his peers. Only the third one is genuinely concerned and listens to them with respect.

Ultimately, he is the one most able to influence others as he shows genuine respect and understanding towards them.

What does this anecdote bring out? It illustrates the 'motivations' that we may have when we talk and interact with us. Do we really wish to 'know' a person, hence, 'connect' with them? Are we just being polite, trying to 'network' in common parlance? Or, do we wish to assess them and try to bring out how we are better in some manner? Or, are we truly interested in knowing about them? I never asked Nilesh directly, but I think he correctly picked out that often I did not really 'connect' with people, even as I engaged with them. Maybe I was just greeting them because I had to in a corporate environment. I was perhaps too judgmental at times, trying to assess them and their possible contributions to a project. All this made me aloof and disconnected.

I still affect many in a similar way, though I feel I have become a bit better in recent times. Certainly, a senior person from Human Resources of my most recent organization complemented me for taking time to engage with people and find out about them. Well, the story helped!

In fact, there is also a story in the *Panchatantra* with a similar theme. Four brahmins lived in a village and were great childhood friends. Three of them spent most of their time studying the sacred texts and other books of knowledge but the fourth, who was regarded as a dullard, spent most of his time like the other simple folk in the village.

One day, the three scholars decided that that all their accomplishments and learning were pointless if they did not use it to show their prowess to others and gain the respect of the folk around them, and in turn, also gain some political power and money. The three at first were reluctant to take the fourth friend along, but one of them felt that they should not leave their childhood friend behind, hence, all decided to travel together.

They started on their journey and soon came upon a large forest. While passing through it, they spotted a number of bones on the path, which appeared to be those of a dead lion. One of them said, 'Here is a chance to show off how learned and skilled we are! Let us bring the lion back to life through our superior knowledge.'

The first said, 'I can assemble the bones of the lion into a complete skeleton.' The second said, 'If you do that, I can add on the muscles and skin.' The third said, 'Once you do that, I can give it life.'

But the fourth, who was a man of no scholarship said, 'No please! Don't try such a thing. These are the bones of a lion, the ferocious king of the forest. If you bring it to life it will kill every one of us.'

The other three grew angry. They said to the fourth, 'It was a mistake to bring you along. You can contribute nothing and are merely jealous of us and wish to deny us this opportunity to show and test our learning. We will not let it go.'

'Very well,' replied the fourth. 'Do as you wish, but first let me climb this tree. And don't forget that I had warned you.'

The three learned friends each demonstrated their fantastic abilities one by one. Needless to say, once the third had completed his efforts, the lion roared into life and immediately attacked the three scholars, killing them quickly. Only the fourth friend, a simpleton, with little scholarship but plenty of common sense, survived.

The morals of this anecdote are many. First, as I have said before in this chapter, it is important to listen to others and show respect.

Second, one must think before performing an action. Particularly, think about the motive and the consequences of the action. Is it an action performed just for showing off one's capabilities or for other selfish motives? Or will it help someone? Will it bring some good or some change for the better?

Relating to this, I would also advise people that if they have a strong urge to do something, always stop and think about what is the real reason for wanting to do so. One must always seek to understand and be honest about one's own motives.

My NCERT textbooks when I was in school always had a page at the beginning, with 'Gandhiji's talisman'. The Mahatma had suggested that whenever one was in doubt or was contemplating an action, one should recall the face of the poorest or weakest individual he/she had seen. Would the proposed action help that person? Would it enable him/her to take control of life and destiny? Gandhiji said that once one had these thoughts, one's doubts, and more importantly, one's self fades away.

Another aspect the story reveals is that those in power should not discard or disrespect the 'minority' voice or an alternate opinion. There is much value in contrarian thinking. I can personally testify about it. The founder of an oil firm, where I had worked, described his company's strategy as 'sensibly contrarian'. Hence, it is essential to think about doing what others did not and avoid doing what everyone does. There is much to be gained from listening to and respecting those with different opinions.

NEVER UNDERESTIMATE THE POWER OF HUMILITY

A recent Forbes article points out the need to possess humility amongst leaders. Dr Robert Hogan, founder and president of Hogan Assessments, observed, 'Substantial research shows that humility predicts effective leadership. Humility is associated with minimizing status differences, listening to subordinates, soliciting input, admitting mistakes and being willing to change course when a plan seems not to work.'[1]

Jim Collins' famous work *Good to Great*, which looked at several hundred companies in the Fortune 500 list of companies over a 30-year period. Collins looked for those organizations that had been performing at or around the market, on an average for at least 15 years before a transition point, after which they outperformed the market by at least three times for the next 15 years. He aimed to understand what aspects made the crucial difference in companies that enabled them to move from 'good to great' and sustain that greatness. He outlined two distinct characteristics among the leaders of these companies—humility and a steely determination to do the right thing for the company, no matter how difficult, that is, going beyond one's own self-interest and looking at the good of the company as a whole.

A later study was conducted by Ou, Waldman and Peterson, entitled, 'Do humble CEOs matter?'[2] This study of 105 IT companies, where the CEOs depicted greater humility, also

---

[1] K. Higginbottom, 'The Value of Humility in Leadership', *Forbes*, July 2018. https://www.forbes.com/sites/karenhigginbottom/2018/07/18/the-value-of-humility-in-leadership/#aff57db24e99.

[2] Amy Y. Ou, David A. Waldman and Suzanne J. Peterson, 'Do Humble CEOs Matter? An Examination of CEO Humility and Firm Outcomes', *Journal of Management* 44, no. 3 (21 September 2015): 1147–1173. https://doi.org/10.1177/0149206315604187.

demonstrated greater leadership, team integration, collaboration and cooperation and flexibility in strategic orientation. So how can you recognize humility and practice it? What kind of behaviour should you exhibit?

Humble leaders listen to feedback and are willing to acknowledge mistakes, therefore, make a course correction if a decision turns out to be wrong. Hence, they try to listen and invite people to voice their ideas and challenges.

Adrian Lock, a senior consultant and programme leader for strategic leadership at Roffey Park Institute, provides some tips for leaders wishing to practice more humility[3]:

- Be curious, he says; and never stop being a learner. Spend time listening and learning from those at the front line of your business and those with very different life experiences to your own.

- Seek feedback regularly; treat it as a gift and act on it. Develop your awareness of your strengths and weaknesses so that you know when to ask for help from others.

- Be authentic—own up to mistakes and apologize when your behaviour or decision-making falls below standard. Honesty consistently comes out on the top when people are asked about their most important values. People do not need a perfect leader but they gladly follow one who owns up to mistakes.

- Give up the need to have all the right answers; focus on asking the right questions.

---

[3] Higginbottom, The Value Of Humility.

The last point is extremely crucial. It means moving away from being seen as an 'expert' oneself and trying to bring about the expertise and competence of others. This is really what makes one a leader, but being able to bring out the expertise of others is no mean task.

I will draw this chapter to a close with two stories about George Washington, the first President of the United States of America; while the stories may be apocryphal, they are worth pondering over.

Help Out, Not Order

Once upon a time, George Washington was riding when he came across a few soldiers who were trying to move a heavy log of wood from a roadside, but without much success. The leader of the group of men was a corporal, who was standing by just watching as the men struggled.

The rider couldn't believe what he saw and asked the corporal why he was not helping and just standing by idly.

The corporal replied, 'I am the corporal. I give orders.'

The rider said nothing in response. Instead, he dismounted from his horse and went up to the log and tried to lift the wood with the other men. With this extra bit of help, the task was finally accomplished.

George Washington, at the time, was the commander-in-chief of the armed forces. He now quietly mounted his horse and went to the corporal and said, 'The next time your men need help, send for the commander-in-chief.'

***

Once George Washington was riding near Washington city with a group of friends and they came to a place where they had to leap over a wall. In the process, one horse knocked off a number of stones from the wall.

Washington said, 'We better replace them.'

His friends replied, 'Oh, let the farmer do it.'

But George Washington didn't feel right about this. When the riding party was over, he went back the way they came.

He found the wall and dismounted. Then he carefully replaced each of the stones.

His riding companion saw what he did and said, 'You're too big to do that.'

He responded, 'On the contrary, I am the right size.'

So the next time, do stop and listen and show respect to all individuals, irrespective of their education level or background. People from diverse backgrounds offer different perspectives and sometimes by doing things differently, it can lead to radically different outcomes.

People around you sometimes can give you an idea, which you can develop into a huge success. Ideas come from anywhere, but keeping one's ears to the ground to pick these up is important.

Chapter 3

Going to Gemba

There are no old roads to new directions.
—Anonymous

All of us have seen a detective movie at some time or the other. Try and recall the very first thing the detective does when he gets to know about a major crime such as a murder. What is it that comes to mind? I think most of us know the answer. The first thing the detective does is that he/she visits the crime scene. In fact, the detective may get a call at 2 AM about a murder. He/she generally drops everything he/she is doing or immediately gets out of bed (depending on the time) and goes to the crime scene. Why is this so?

This is because the investigation must start from the place of action. This is where the clues to solving the crime could be found. The detective should thus go to the scene of action immediately; for there may be some smell, some way in which the light comes into the room...something, however small, that the detective notices which later could help him solve the crime.

Indeed, I can recall two detective stories where the quick eye of the detective was essential. In one, the detective gets a clue from the way in which the curtains on one of the windows were drawn. In another, the detective notices something about a footprint outside one of the windows—it was incongruous with the weather, hence, the detective realizes it must have been deliberately planted there.

In fact, Crime Scene Investigation (or CSI) is a highly specialized branch of criminology, so much so, that a popular television series *CSI: Crime Scene Investigation* (also called *CSI: Las Vegas*), ran for as many as 15 years on CBS, from October 2000 to September 2015, spanning 15 seasons.

The series follows a team of crime scene investigators employed by the Las Vegas Police Department, as they use physical evidence at the crime scene to solve murders. I particularly remember an episode where the police are searching high and low for the murder weapon. Meanwhile, all the evidence points to a particular individual who had visited the victim a few hours before she had been murdered. The crime scene investigator looks carefully all around the scene of the murder and finally realizes that the victim had been strangulated by the curtain rope-which is still hanging around the curtain. The investigator uses epithelial cells from this to extract DNA and the entire evidence is turned on its head as it points to the presence of a third person.

The bottom line is that visiting the crime scene, often more than once, is crucial to solve the mystery. No detective, whether in fiction or real life, can wish to solve a mystery sitting in his office and speculating; and no lazy policemen can solve a murder by squatting in a police station. You have to go out to the place where the action is/has taken place.

In the world of management, I have seen many management consultants from reputed firms doing no better than a lazy detective or police officer (let me be the first to admit that I have also been employed with some of these organizations and have made this mistake at times, more so in the early part of my career).

They often sit around, having innumerable meetings which they term as brainstorming sessions, where they sit around and bandy ideas. Very often, these sessions are just used to air speculative thoughts on what could be going on.

Of course, most consulting firms do back these sessions up by looking at data but trying to solve a company's problem merely by looking at numbers on an excel sheet is NOT the right way to solve real-life problems.

Data and numbers on an excel sheet is subject to the viewer's interpretation, thus, involves one's biases, fears and assumptions. More importantly, they do not carry any 'notes to aid interpretation'. Two different people looking at the same data can draw different conclusions.

If you don't agree with this, think of two cricket captains at the time of the toss. Both have a similar set of data to consider—the pitch, pitch conditions, weather forecast and so on, and having considered all this, both may reach completely opposite conclusions; one captain might feel that it is best to bat first on the pitch, while the other might think it is best to bowl first. This is a dramatic illustration for it considers two conclusions poles apart—to bat or to bowl first. However, it serves to explain the point—that is, data is always subject to interpretation. Or put in different words, data is subject to speculative interpretation.

How then does one solve a business problem or issue? The answer is simple—follow the method of the sprightly investigator, go to the crime scene and then apply the method, as Sherlock Holmes would do.

In business jargon, go to the place where value addition occurs. This is where the customer is making his purchases; the logistics supervisor is directing loading or unloading, the shop-floor supervisor is performing his activity, it is the place where the action is taking place.

MANY SURPRISES AWAIT AT THE SCENE OF ACTION

You cannot understand issues properly or solve issues by looking at numbers in an excel. So get off your backside and go to the field of action.

I had the fortune of beginning my career at HUL, India's largest fast moving consumer goods (FMCG) firm (called at the time Hindustan Lever Ltd or HLL). Like many others, I thus began my career 'selling soap' as former HUL executives like to put it; though apart from selling soaps and detergents, we also sold cosmetics and other products.

There were a number of remarkable things one noticed while being in the actual market. One of HUL's biggest and most well-known brands (and also, perhaps the most controversial) was Fair & Lovely (FAL). The product promised to 'lighten' the user's complexion if used regularly.

The product was in every way, clearly targeted at women. Its advertising always showed women using it the colour of the packaging had a great degree of pink in it. The 'Fair & Lovely Foundation' was almost completely meant for women, offering scholarships, career guidance and advice to them. The company stated that its research claims that '90 per cent of Indian women want to use whiteners because it is aspirational, like losing weight'.

In spite of this clear focus on the gentler sex, HUL executives began to notice a strange fact: close to 40 per cent of the product's sales, especially in certain geographies, were to men! (Clearly the desire to look fair was not limited to the opposite sex).

So pervasive was this contrarian usage that many companies decided to come up with products especially meant to satisfy the male desire for fairness. Emami launched a competitive product targeted at men with the brand name 'Fair and Handsome'. Bollywood superstar Shahrukh Khan was used to extensively promote this male fairness cream.

To specifically target the male population, in 2006, HUL itself launched a product it called 'Fair & Lovely Men', which was later renamed as 'Men's Fair & Lovely'. Later, Garnier came up with another similar product—'Men Powerlight'.

One of the flagship products of another famous Indian firm, Godrej, was its black hair dye. The first product the company launched in this category was way back in 1974 and was called 'Godrej Liquid Hair Dye'.

Packaged in bottles, this product was a success, so much so that the company was to claim that the term 'hair dye' itself had become synonymous with Godrej; and laid the foundation for the company to become the number one player in the hair colour market. But feedback from the ground had something interesting to say about the product. A not so insignificant percentage of Godrej Hair Dye went towards blackening the skin of buffaloes, especially before cattle fairs!

Washing machines in Punjab were used to make 'lassi' (buttermilk). Further, many shops were too small to accommodate washing machines. So some shopkeepers took a table fan shaft, modified it and added blades to make portable blenders.

These are well-known facts among the executives of the companies in question. Yet, they cannot be gleaned by looking at data and numbers in sheets upon sheets of Microsoft Excel. Visits to the market reveal the truth—and the reasons—behind the numbers. It tells you what is going on and why.

Recently, one of my students came to me, wishing to take his business forward. He had opened a couple of stores that sold fresh beverages such as juices, flavoured milk, and so on. He had done the right thing by speaking to a few individuals in this line of business.

The first thing I advised him was to go and spend a few hours at various juice parlours, quietly observing their patrons. Make notes on his observations. What kind of clientele did these parlours get? What kind of flavours did people order? How did they order? Did they first check the menu and prices before ordering? Did they read the packaging on the bottle? What comments did they make about the product? Did they come in groups or were they primarily single or couples?

Doing this made him realize a few aspects that were important to the business:

- Most juice purchases were spontaneous, especially on hot days. This made him realize that visibility and location of the outlet would be extremely crucial.

- Tastes differed at different locations. In some parlours, for example, mango was the bestselling; while in others it was watermelon.

- Many of those who opted for 'flavoured milk' later wished they had ordered the fresh juices instead.

What I have aimed to highlight in this chapter is not completely new. Many enlightened executives have often known it. HUL made sure that all its new entrants (indeed people far more senior as well) spent as much time as they could in the market. This after all is the place where the action takes place, value is being added and the consumer makes his purchases.

From the perspective of a management philosophy, this is not too different from the old Japanese concept of 'Going to Gemba'. Gemba is where the action is. The Japanese, especially Toyota executives, were told to make sure they spent time there, making sure they observed and understood before making suggestions or speculations. Executives were instructed to go on a 'Gemba walk'.

Consider, for example, the result of the General Elections in India in 2019. The ruling party, the Bharatiya Janata Party (BJP) won what could be termed as a landslide victory, obtaining over 300 seats on its own steam, surprising almost all the analysts in the country who had predicted that the party would fall short of a majority and would win lesser seats than it did in the previous election, five years ago.

What was even more remarkable was that elections in three crucial states—Rajasthan, Madhya Pradesh and Chhattisgarh —had been held only a few months earlier. The opposition Congress(I) Party staged a comeback and won in all the three states.

Analysts were quick to point to a Congress revival, extrapolating the seats won in the state elections to predict how many seats the party would win in the ensuing general elections. All these predictions and analyses totally bit the dust once the general election results actually came in.

I have used this example to illustrate the pitfalls of analysis based on data. It involves many an interpretation, assumption and extrapolation. The data analyst who uses this approach relies on approximations and his assumptions have been correct.

But in reality, real life does not go according to extrapolation of data sets. This is the mistake that consultants and many data analysts make. One has to do a lot more. One has to understand the underlying sentiment, emotion, reality, which underpins the numbers.

How many times have I seen firms taking this year's demand and adding a few percentage points to estimate that of next year? The same is done the following year. While such estimates may approximate reality when taken over a long period of years (for deviations smoothen themselves out), but the estimated figures for the next particular year are way off mark.

Consider one possibility as to how data estimations go wrong, very often as a result of a successful promotional activity, and the sales of an FMCG go up in a particular quarter. Management extrapolates the same growth to subsequent quarters and uses the charts to attract shareholders and investors. When the next quarter begins, however, the numbers begin to reflect a different picture. Leave aside growth, the sales actually diminish from the previous quarter. Investors beat down the stock and management starts panicking.

If they had understood the ground reality, they would have realized that successful promotion meant that many customers (read retailers or the end consumer as the case may be) had pushed forward their purchase of the FMCG product to the previous quarter to take advantage of the promotion; hence, they have enough stock of the product left in the next quarter. This is the classical fallacy that is often seen. A one-time positive result is misinterpreted as the start of a trend. Such mistakes (both assuming the start of a trend when there is none as well as failing to notice a trend) can be avoided by 'Going to Gemba' rather than relying on only interpretation of numbers.

'GO SEE, ASK WHY, SHOW RESPECT'

It is worth dwelling more on this philosophy. What is it and how should it be done?

The words of former Toyota Chairman, Fujio Cho, 'Go see, ask why, show respect,' are now famous. These words show the way in which the philosophy of scientific empiricism can be translated into actual behaviour. We can go observe what is really happening (and not speculate or think what might or could be happening), and seek to understand.

Such a visit and effort gives us two major opportunities:

- Helps to separate fact from the fiction
- Identify the facts and question dangerous assumptions and beliefs that can make one go astray

What do we wish to do when we 'Go to Gemba'? The idea is to understand every activity which adds value from the standpoints of purpose, process and people.

Consider the following:

- Is the management working to align people and processes to achieve the defined purpose?

- Are the processes, then designed, enable people to achieve the organizational purpose—the 'why' of the organization (refer to my chapter in this book on more about the 'why').

- Are people engaged in working to achieve the purpose, and are they supported in this work by the processes?

Having understood the purpose of the organization, a person on the 'Gemba walk' (it could be a company executive or a management consultant) then focuses on the process-related aspects. He asks questions and makes observations, noting these down if necessary.

It is important during this stage to 'show respect', which means that one should refrain from making suggestions or directing people. First understand what is happening and why, rather than jumping in with comments or your own perspective.

Related to this, is to identify where the concept of Kaizen can be placed. Kaizen, as most of us already know, means 'continuous improvement'. But how do we ensure this? Taiichi Ohno, assumed to be the father of the Toyota Production System (TPS), was absolutely right when he observed that one's mindset needs to be attuned towards this. One must welcome mistakes, for they represent a chance to be still better, to improve to a higher level.

To observe with this view towards Kaizen, I suggest you start your observations as close as possible to the customer; then work your way back. Do the processes align with the needs of the customer? Think later if they can be improved to serve the customer better.

For example, when I spoke about impulse purchasing being important in the business of selling juices, clearly the processes must be aligned. Hence, juice parlours must be able to quickly make fresh juices for the customer wants freshly prepared juices or prepared recently and often in front of his eyes, especially in a country such as India, so that the customer feels assured that no artificial additives or poor quality water is being used.

If one was to consider the final delivery to the customer and his need of a high quality, good tasting, fresh product, try to look for any possible disruption to this, for example, quality variations due to overburdening any of the people involved in the process. You may have noticed on a particular day, in a restaurant which normally serves delectable food, the food is less tasty- and this is often on a day when the restaurant has more customers than usual.

A very important concept while on Gemba is to 'do no harm'. Put in other words, people around you should welcome your efforts, for it may help remove an obstacle to their work, making them more productive or effective. The Gemba walk is not a time for fault-finding or recriminations. If used negatively, people will not be their usual selves. While you seek to understand, they will merely put on a show meant to impress you. Since this does not reflect their usual behaviour, the exercise becomes pointless.

This phenomenon manifests itself often when senior politicians visit a site or indeed when CEOs or top management go on field visits. Everything is made to go like clockwork but that is not the everyday reality.

The real purpose of this philosophy is to allow managers and leaders to observe the actual work process, engage with employees, gain knowledge about work process and explore opportunities for continuous improvement. The Gemba walk is not a 'boss walk'. It is a colleague's walk. It is there to find faults in the process, not in people. And remember, that the senior management, that is, you yourself, are often responsible for faults in the processes, at least indirectly.

HOW CAN YOU BE EFFECTIVE WHILE GOING TO GEMBA?

As an aid, I am outlining some thoughts towards making your effort to 'go to the crime scene' or the place where the action takes place more effective:

- **You Could Pick up a Theme:** Try and choose one particular theme that will help you to focus all your efforts. Different aspects that could be the theme:
  o Better customer service
  o Improving productivity
  o Cost efficiency
  o Process efficiency
  o Health and safety

  For the first few times, I strongly suggest you prepare a list of questions you would like to ask.

  In case there is a problem to solve, you could start by defining the problem. Write down a problem statement. This may not always be easy and often people underestimate how important this stage is, so they either skip it assuming they understand the problem or they attack the problems with vague ideas, beliefs and assumptions. Worse still, people often generalize excessively, for example, by stating that the energy consumption of a factory is too high, rather than looking into what exactly is causing this high consumption.

To avoid this, use the 5Ws. These simple questions will help you to define your problem statement:

o Who: Who does the problem affect? In the example above, does the high consumption affect the occupants of the building or the building owners or facility management companies (elevators or HVAC companies, and so on)?

o What: What is the extent of the problem?

o When: When does the problem occur? Certain days only? Certain seasons? Or throughout?

o Where: Where does the issue occur?

o Why: Why is it important to solve this? What impact will it have?

- **Focus on Process, Not on People:** As mentioned before, the Gemba walk is not the time for evaluating the performance of your team. The main purpose is to observe, understand and improve the process. If you focus on people's personal capabilities or shortcomings, you will only face resistance or people will put on a 'show' for you, negating the purpose of the walk.

- **Follow the Value Chain:** Following the value chain will give you the best opportunities to identify areas with a high potential of waste activities. Eliminating those activities will help you improve the overall performance.

As I said earlier, you could start with the customer and watch what he wants and how he orders/consumes the product, and work backwards from there; trying to eliminate those aspects that are unimportant and addressing those that are relevant.

- **Record Your Observations Carefully but Avoid Making Suggestions during the Walk:** Write down everything that grabs your attention; in today's world you can do it electronically or even record it with your smartphone. Don't offer a solution immediately, even if you are tempted; leave the analysis for later. You will be much more accurate with your solutions after you have all the facts available.

- **Ask to See Examples of What You May Have Been Told Earlier:** Remember that one solid piece of evidence is worth more than lots of statements or numbers in MS Excel. It is certainly worth a lot more than possibilities and speculations. When I suggest you ask to see the reality, this is also a great opportunity to bust any assumptions or false theories that might be floating around.

- **Question 'Round' Numbers, or Numbers That Seem to Be Convenient:** What seems to be convenient may actually be based on judgements or vague remembrances rather than facts. Seek the actual numbers. For example, try and see how many pieces of an item a machine actually produces in one hour. If someone says approximately 100, question it; such a number is just too convenient.

- **Envision What an 'Ideal Process' Might Look Like:** See how the actual or real process is different or falls short of the ideal. If you know of a similar process that runs better, use that as a reference.

For example, there is a particular heath service pro-vider in India—Aravind Eye Clinic—who is able to perform several more cataract and other eye surgeries than any other eye hospital in India. This is a fantastic opportunity of 'Going to Gemba'. Any healthcare consultant should go and actually see how they manage this- rather than just look at the data and make guesses. There is much learning to be made from actually witnessing their processes and procedures.

- **After the Walk:** Even if you don't find anything significant during your visit/Gemba walk, you need to share with the people what you have observed and learned or seen. Otherwise, they will only have the feeling of being watched. If you are going to take actions after the walk, inform the teams what you have observed about the upcoming changes and why they are necessary.

I would, hence, strongly advise all senior executives, especially those in roles where they have to contribute ideas or strategy, to spend time 'at the source'. It is from people at the point that value is being added and one gets a lot of incredible suggestions. However, sometimes, these people may lack the opportunity, the skill or finesse to put across these ideas properly, and that is where you come in.

For example, it is always worth speaking to a few waiters when advising a restaurant chain. They know the customer the best and what he/she expects or asks for. Similarly, speak to truck drivers to understand matters pertaining to logistics. Involve those from the shop-floor in discussions about production optimization.

Chapter 4

A Thousand Songs in Your Pocket: What Jobs Did Right

It was a hot summer in the year 2004 and I was fresh out of IIM Calcutta and had just started my job with HUL, the country's largest FMCG firm, as part of the company's fabled training programme for fresh graduates.

All of us, the young students, were taken through various stints as part of this training programme, during which we were called 'Business Leadership Trainees' (BLTs). We were told to observe whatever we noticed in the market about the company, its marketing and advertising methods, competitors and their strategies, etc., and make careful notes.

One of the first aspects that we observed was the advertising of HUL's popular and controversial brand, Fair and Lovely. The advertisements stated that the product was a skin lightening cream and helped the user look fairer after just a couple of weeks of usage. The advertisements also portrayed a young woman, who was earlier rejected for something (it could be in a job interview or a role in a movie), changing her fate after using the product.

This sort of advertising made the product extremely controversial and there were many who criticized such a depiction, stating that it promoted stereotypes, reinforced the typical Indian predilection for fairness, etc., with some NGOs even suggesting the product should be boycotted.

The product itself continued to sell heavily, being one of the first FMCG products to cross the ₹1,000 crore mark in sales alone. This was no mean feat, for it meant that this single product brought in more revenues than that of all the products of many of HUL's competitors put together.

The company was thus unfazed with the barrage of criticism it received for the nature of its advertising, largely ignoring the analysis and at times responding by pointing out that it had not created the Indian preference for fair skin but merely reflected the already extant desire that Indian consumers possessed to look 'fairer'.

I often thought about the product's advertising strategy. Gradually, I noticed that this form of advertising was not used by HUL just for its fairness cream, but for many others, including its other flagship brands in the soaps and detergents category.

Lifebuoy, India's largest selling soap, was promoted as a germ killer and something that ensured that one's hands were clean. The company went so far as to convince people, especially in rural areas, through innovative methods of the change that the use of the soap brought—asking them to pass their hands through a device which showed them just how many germs and bacteria their hands had before and after using the product.

Liril, was sold with the promise of making the user feel fresh (remember the famous 'Girl in the Waterfall' advertisement that helped make Lintas' Alyque Padamsee a household name); Lux was sold as a beauty bar; and Rin, the company's flagship detergent was sold with the promise that it would remove stains and make your clothes look spotlessly white.

Put together, I saw that the company had got its advertising methods right as they were direct and spoke to the audience about the benefits without sugar coating or complicating it.

LEVITT AND HIS HOLES

Theodore Levitt (March 1925-June 2006) was a well-known American economist and a famous professor at the Harvard Business School. He was editor of the *Harvard Business Review* (*HBR*), and was noted for both popularizing the publication as well as the term globalization. But he is perhaps best known for his article 'Marketing Myopia' that appeared in the *HBR* way back in 1959.

A famous marketing professor at Harvard, Levitt used to outline his marketing concepts to his class and then summarize his concept with the following succinct line: 'People don't want to buy a quarter-inch drill. They want a quarter-inch hole.' This is a truth that every marketer, every company and every advertiser must never forget.

First, it is not the product that the customer wants; it is the use of the product that appeals him/her. A consumer, therefore, does not want to buy toothbrushes; he wants to keep his teeth clean. Do not think he has some special love for his toothbrushes, in reality, he loves his teeth. Similarly when he buys a drill bit, the consumer wants something that gets the job done, quickly and most efficiently. He does not really care about the material of the drilling tool or its length. Put in different words, the consumer actually cares about the holes that the drill will help him/her to make. Based on this simple insight, the marketing and positioning of the product should focus on the quality of the holes, and not the features of the product.

Second, the product is only a means to an end. The consumer will be happy to buy anything that meets his need. If he wants to quench his thirst, for example, you cannot expect him only to buy a soft drink. He/she may reach for a juice, a 'nimbupani' or just plain water, Coke realized this explicitly when they said their biggest competitor is not Pepsi, but drinking water. Hence, the company came up with a famous punchline '*Thanda matlab Coca-Cola*'. When the user is thirsty and wants refreshment, he should think of a Coca-Cola.

This recognition of what the consumer really wants is essential. He does NOT, for example, need your company's watch if his real need is to tell the time. He gets to know the time from his mobile phone in today's world. On the other hand, if you are selling premium watches, he may meet his need for status through some other premium product.

SELL BENEFITS, NOT FEATURES

The bottom line is that you have to make a product that meets the need of a customer and then tell him how the product benefits him or her. In other words, 'Benefits sell, features don't'.

What does this really mean? In simple terms, all your marketing messaging should focus on and communicate the benefits of your product and not its features to potential customers. It sounds logical, but it is not always done. Why? Many a time, companies and their executives get carried away with what they have made and assume that the customer cares about this. Harping on features would be to put the cart before the horse. Consumers care about features if and only if, they understand the tangible benefits that they get. What the consumer really wants to know is: 'What is in it for me?' 'How is this feature going to make a difference to me?' 'Will it make my life better or easier or more convenient?'

What does this mean in practical terms? Consider the following examples and decide what you think is more effective among the following set of statements:

- 'A Maruti car provides 1.5 km/litre mileage than its competitor'

  vs

  'Save money when you drive a Maruti'
- 'Buy our cooking books with glossy paper and 50 recipes'

vs

'Thrill your friends and relatives with our recipes'

- 'Our light bulbs provide better light'

  vs

  'Save your eyesight by using our light bulbs'

- 'Our book on how to lose weight has 200 pages of content with many illustrations. It has many diets you can choose from and a comprehensive list of exercises'

  vs

  'Start losing weight in the next two days; read about 25 exercises that will melt away your fat and help you lose 5 kg in a week'

- 'The tread on our tyres lasts for 20,000 km'

  vs

  'Our tyres keep you safe'

- Our new titanium drill bit'

  vs

  'Our new drill bit helps you drill faster'

- 'Our sleeping bag has an additional insulation layer'

  vs

  'Our sleeping bag helps retain body heat. So wake up well rested even on cold nights'

- 'Our software automates supply chains'

  vs

  'Our software makes your products available for sale 20 per cent faster'

- 'We provide fast internet connections'

  vs

  'Get directions faster when you are lost' or 'download movies faster'

- 'Our software makes you more productive'

  vs

  'Our customers report an average 25 per cent decrease in costs, about one and a half times better than the industry average'

- 'Home delivery offered'

  vs

  'Save 30 minutes daily by using our home delivery service'

- 'Contains an artificial intelligence algorithm'

  vs

  'Adapts to and customizes the user's information experience'

And coming to HUL's products, what sounds better? Stating that

- 'Our product has ingredients such as sorbitol, glycerine, etc.'

  vs

  'Freshens your breath and fights cavities'

You would have likely felt that the second option was more impactful. In all these cases, it is because the second option in the various sets stress on the benefits of using the product. What difference does it really make to the user?

There are some who take this concept further and say that customers don't even want to own the product. In a way, they just want to use it or hire it to accomplish a certain task or solve a certain problem. Hence, your marketing must focus on that task or problem and how your product can solve the problem, instead of focusing on the product itself.

Hence, Fair and Lovely's key message would always be how it helped the user—lightened her skin thus increasing her confidence and helping her get a certain role or a job—and not on the ingredients or constituents of the product itself.

So the next time you think about your marketing campaign, remember it does not matter what your product or service does. It does not matter what you have developed with so much effort and sweat. What really matters is the little way in which the product can or its service will improve users' lives.

Let us take a step back here and examine the concepts in greater detail.

What Is a Feature?

Put in simple terms, a feature is something that your product or service has or is. Product features might include, for example,

- Razors with three blades
- Refrigerators that can make crushed ice
- A software program that uses AI, etc.
- An umbrella with wind-resistant spokes
- 1 GB storage

What Is a Benefit?

Benefits are the outcomes or results that consumers will experience by using your product or service.

What are the benefits in the above cases?

- Getting a better shave that helps you look more handsome
- Getting ice quickly that is ready to use
- Getting more accurate and faster results
- An umbrella that ensures you stay dry even in strong winds
- Getting 1,000 songs in your device or a 100 videos

Marketers often confuse the two; for having spent a lot of time on research and understanding consumer issues, they forget that to the ordinary person, the benefits of using their product may not be immediately obvious. Put in another way, just because a company knows what's great about its product doesn't mean that the consumer does.

There is another reason as well. Often companies equate the time and effort that went into developing a new feature with its importance to consumers. They feel that if they went through long hours of feature conceptualization, testing and implementation, it will have a big impact on consumers. It might, but only if the consumer realizes how it will make some difference to her life.

For example, one advertisement, typically shown on television, spoke about a 48-inch television with 1080p high definition. Now this is the classical trap. No attempt is being made to portray the benefits of your product or service. Why does the customer need a 48-inch television with 1080p high definition? If you fail to explain it to him, he may well settle for a smaller (and cheaper) set with lower resolution.

The marketer here has largely failed to speak to the customer in the language a customer would understand; in reality, the customer does not even need to understand what '1080p high definition' is, as long as you explain the benefits. You have to tell the customer how he or she will be better off with those features, or how a feature will make their lives different, i.e., the way he will see value in going for a larger (and costlier) television set.

Guerilla Marketing in 30 Days, written by Jay Conrad Levinson (the man who is said to have founded the concept of guerrilla marketing) and Al Lautenslager describes features as factual statements about a product or service. Some factual statements that are often confused with benefits include examples such as:

- 'Self-cleaning oven'
- '200-CD jukebox'
- 'One-click buying on Amazon'
- 'Live operator on duty 24/7'
- '125-page owner's manual included'
- 'In business since 1910'
- 'We have the biggest widget maker'
- 'Award-winning'
- 'Made with 100 per cent recycled product'

However, most customers care little about these statements and are not really influenced by them, for the simple reason that none of these examples really tells a prospective consumer how their life or work will improve as a result of buying your product or service. Of course, they could appeal to a relatively small segment of people; for example, the fact that a product has been recycled could appeal those who are extremely conscious of the environment.

The latest and even best equipment or technology means nothing to a prospective buyer unless that feature translates into something that he cares about. It could be increased productivity, or lower costs or quicker delivery or anything else that he values.

Many companies state how long they have been in business; for example, some may mention 'since 1910'. This means nothing until that fact can be translated into a benefit of reliability and a guarantee of being in business in the future.

Let's try our hand at flipping the coin, so to speak. Can you transform the facts above into aspects that consumers may value? Build your statements around the following possible benefits to the consumer:

- Convenience
- Time saving
- Easy access
- Quicker delivery
- Faster answers
- Accuracy
- Saving resources required
- Reliability

Consumers wish to know whether the product will make them 'healthier, wealthier or wiser' Speedier answers make them wiser.

Better returns or cost savings make them wealthier. Less of sugar makes them healthier.

Of course, it is also worth remembering here that the most compelling benefits are those that provide emotional or financial return. Emotional returns are related to making the customer feel better in some way. Financial returns generally save money or make money for a customer.

On the other hand, features are often couched in a jargon that a layman (the average customer) finds difficult to comprehend. Does he really understand what a HD or plasma TV does? Over-reliance on such terms could mean that a large portion of the potential customer base simply won't understand the message if nothing but technical specifications are provided; this would place the burden of understanding on the reader.

The customer has to connect the dots between the specifications listed and comprehend how it will actually benefit them. But when he/she is left to draw his/her conclusions, there is a risk of them drawing the wrong ones.

As an example, let us take the case of an automobile company that markets its automobile as being 'fast'. The company probably wants to give a positive message. But the prospective customer could perhaps interpret the vehicle as being 'reckless'; even unsafe.

CHARLES REVSON: THE MERCHANT OF HOPE

One of the best examples I feel of 'selling benefits' is using what Charles Revson had said. Charles Revson was the founder of Revlon, one of the world's largest cosmetics company. Revson very famously said: 'In the factory we make cosmetics. In the store we sell Hope.'

Think of this statement carefully. Revson was so right. His factories made products. But what he sold in his retail stores was certainly not products or their ingredients, however much you may feel that consumers wished to know what secrets there were in the cosmetics. What Revlon sold—and what consumers bought—were 'promises' or 'hope'—the hope that one's skin would remain wrinkle free by using that anti-wrinkle cream; the hope that one would look younger by using that anti-aging combination, etc. The consumer only cared about the end result and the benefits—whether he/she would look better or younger or if his/her skin would glow more, not about what went into the product or the amount of R&D effort that went into it.

A THOUSAND SONGS

Still not convinced? Think of what Steve Jobs did when he first launched the iPod. The device must have required thousands of hours of R&D work, effort and many iterations. The revolutionary device must have had no dearth of features that Jobs could have highlighted to Apple's many aficionados. For example, the original iPod featured a 5 GB hard drive, Firewire connectivity, and synchronization to iTunes. By using a 1.8″ drive, the iPod was significantly smaller than competing MP3 players of the time.

But how did Steve Jobs, the man who exemplified in many ways someone who knew how to marry art and science, choose to market his revolutionary feature-packed device? He used five simple words: '1000 songs in Your Pocket'.

This message was all about the benefits to the end user—he could get more songs in the device than any other competitive offering. No mention of the capacity of the hard drive, no mention of size, etc. Just what it meant to the user; how it made his/ her life different. He could get more songs.

It is said that leading up to the iPod launch in October 2001, Steve Jobs had personally managed the process of deciding on both the name and the message of this breakthrough product. What is noteworthy is that Jobs had apparently decided on the message even before Apple had named the product. The message—'1000 songs in your pocket'—is said to have been clear in his mind some months before the name 'iPod' was chosen from a list of 10 options.

When Jobs stood on stage on October 23, 2001 in front of the world's press and tech analysts, he started by talking about how much he and the people at Apple loved music; and went on to say that the then available set of MP3 players were disappointing.

He then moved on to opine what would make a great MP3 player; this included the key point that it should store a lot of songs—say, 1000—so you wouldn't have to keep syncing it with your computer. Further, it should be small enough to fit in your pocket; and have a user interface that makes it quick and easy to find the song you want.

Then came the punchline: 'Well', said Jobs, 'I have this perfect product right here in my pocket.' He pulled the product out of his front jeans pocket and announced, 'The iPod. 1000 songs in your pocket!'

Immediately, the screen behind him reinforced the message; and within an hour, the Apple homepage was screaming, 'The iPod. 1000 songs in your pocket.'

Hundreds of journalists and reviewers from the audience wrote reviews of the iPod the next day. Needless to say, almost all had the '1000 songs in your pocket' message as either the headline or the key component of the first couple of paragraphs. Those who purchased the product initially also showed it off with the same message. 'Hey, have you seen this new device? 1000 songs in your pocket!'

To understand why this was such a big deal and also the genius of Jobs' messaging, consider the following: the first iPod was about the size of a deck of cards, yet could store the promised thousand songs. It would take as much as a hundred Compact Disks (CDs) to equal the storage of the iPod—so how much easier would it make life for someone who loved music?

Instead of a whole stack of CDs, one needed just a pocket-sized device. People could now carry their entire music library in their pocket! They no longer needed to decide what tapes or CDs they need to take with them because they had their entire music collection with them!

The incredible success of the iPod, along with the later introduction of the iTunes Music Store in June 2003, completely changed the landscape of the music and computer industry. It made music a great deal more personal; but most importantly mobile.

Such an approach which so clearly highlighted the benefit also meant that Apple could indeed command a premium price, as it indeed does for most of its products. After all, the benefits of its products are clear.

WHAT'S BEHIND NANO'S FAILURE

Much has been written about the Nano car. Perhaps the most famous car to be launched by Tata Motors. Ratan Tata, chairman of what is perhaps India's most respected conglomerate, made a public commitment in 2003 to deliver the world's cheapest car, priced at ₹100,000 (roughly USD 2,500) in those days.

Almost the entire world, especially the world's press, picked up Tata's statement and wondered if India's frugal engineering could help Tata deliver his promise. Many were sceptical.

But Tata did deliver; and the Indian press during the launch of the new car at the Automobile Expo in New Delhi in January 2008 screamed out headlines such as 'The World Said No No, but Tata Said Nano' and highlighted Tata's statement that 'A Promise is a Promise'. Tata himself said the launch was the realization of a dream he had had six years ago to create a car cheap enough for Indian families to trade-in their motorbikes.

Despite all the positive press, the Nano proved to be a disaster; something that would have perhaps even sunk a group not as big as the Tatas. Monthly sales never crossed a few thousands, despite the hype that such an attractively priced car could sell in the hundreds of thousands, if not millions; and completely revolutionize the personal mobility sector in India (A 2008 study, by a respected Indian rating agency, for example, thought the Nano would expand the nation's car market by as much as 65 per cent; while the *Telegraph* of the UK mentioned Ratan Tata as stating that he now expected competitors to produce a low-cost rival, but that he believed Tata could sell one million cars a year in India while expanding into developing countries in Africa, Southeast Asia and eventually, Europe and the US[1]).

After a little while, the sales were down to a few hundred per month; and a few tears down the line, the group eventually

[1] Dean Nelson, 'Tata Nano, World's Cheapest Car, Launched in India', *The Telegraph*, 23 March 2009; https://www.telegraph.co.uk/news/worldnews/asia/india/5039397/Tata-Nano-worlds-cheapest-car-launched-in-India.html, accessed on 24 October 2019.

discontinued the product altogether. The *Economic Times* in August 2018 reported that Tata produced just one unit in June 2018, while only three units were sold in the domestic market[2].

What went wrong?

Much has been written about the Nano and its failure. Most analysts and commentators felt it was due to marketing and positioning issues, with consumers hesitant to say they owned 'the world's cheapest car'. After all, especially in economies such as India, a car is a status symbol, and no one wanted to say that he had opted for the cheapest available product.

My personal view is not dissimilar, but links closely to the theme of this chapter. I feel that Ratan Tata got it wrong by constantly highlighting on one *feature*, i.e., the pricing of the car being ₹100,000 and it being the world's cheapest, rather than the *benefits* to the user of owing such a vehicle.

While all Indians may well have been proud that their country had produced such an inexpensive vehicle, particularly of Ratan Tata and celebrated his vision, they did not see the benefits of owning such a product themselves as such details were not communicated.

What the product meant to the consumer was not clear. In fact, the implication that one had bought the world's cheapest car was not a message that a consumer would like to highlight upon. (Ask yourself: would you like to go around saying you have purchased the world's cheapest shirt or even the world's cheapest pen?!). Tata Motors had not communicated enough about the benefits to anyone, including the consumer, or

---

[2] 'Is It End of the Road for Tata's Nano?,' *Economic Times*, 3 August 2018; https://economictimes. indiatimes.com/industry/auto/cars-uvs/is-it-end-of-the-road-for-tatas-nano/no-more-a-peoples-car/ slideshow/64870025.cms, accessed on 24 October 2019.

even respond by saying, 'Yes, it is the world's cheapest, but it offers....'

While I do not wish to appear presumptuous, yet focusing on the benefits of such a product being developed with 'frugal engineering' would have helped much more. Ratan Tata himself later reportedly felt that the product could have been sold to the people who rode on two-wheelers with the whole family as an all-weather safe form of affordable transportation.

Contrast Nano being the cheapest car with Steve Jobs' approach with the iPod. As mentioned, his engineers, just like the ones at Tata's without doubt, would have spent hours and hours of effort to come up with their revolutionary product. Yet Jobs did not get carried away with the product. Even before the product was ready, he was clear on what it would mean for the consumer and what benefit it offered the consumer—a 1000 songs in his pocket. That was the difference.

I do not claim to have identified the reason behind Nano's failure. It is difficult to isolate any one particular reason as being 'the' reason, for successes (and failures) are often due to a combination of factors, including capabilities, strategy, timing and luck. However, this example does advance a viewpoint seen through many experiences on the field and during strategy formulation.

AI PRACTITIONERS BEWARE: DON'T GET CARRIED AWAY BY YOUR TECHNOLOGY

The examples outlined earlier are particularly relevant for the practitioners of Artificial Intelligence (AI) today. Many new companies and products advertise the use of AI or Virtual and Augmented Reality (VR/AR) as if they were ends in themselves.

Very often, the benefits of using AI, AR and VR are not too clear to potential users. This makes the incorporation of such technologies appear faddish, 'the flavour of the season'. Rather, companies using technologies should learn from Steve Jobs' marketing technique. They should emphasize what the technology *does*, not what it is. How will it make a difference to the user? How will it change his life?

Aspects that could be highlighted include getting more accurate outputs, better or faster information, more customized, hence, relevant inputs, etc. The AI and related technologies so used should make something faster, better or more efficient. They should not be incorporated just to 'go with the flow' or make it appear fashionable but with no tangible benefit that could be sold to the customer.

A colleague and I were working on what could be India's first fully AI-powered website for the media house that I was employed with. AI would select the videos, process them, edit them and even provide the synopsis and classification of the videos.

When we took it to a senior executive of the company, he was clear enough, correctly, to feel that the new website would work only if it provided a clear selling point based on the benefit that the viewer would derive—he could get more customized news, or news earlier than anyone else, or more accurate news, etc. Few would want the news just because it was 'completely powered by AI'.

Wherever AI (or new technologies in general) have succeeded, it is when they have clear, compelling benefits for the user and have helped make a difference to the individual or entity using them.

Indeed, AI is reshaping the progress of many sectors today; and is perhaps the most important technology for the 'general purpose' of our times. The effects of AI will be to continue to expand manifold in the coming decade as the sectors of manufacturing, media and entertainment, retail (especially e-commerce), advertising, finance, healthcare, insurance, education, etc., are being impacted by this technology, the usage of which is spreading gradually from the developed nations of the West to India.

One sector that has been majorly impacted is finance. Let us consider the phenomenon of algorithmic trading, which uses software and computers to run complex mathematical formulas combined with mathematical models and human oversight for trading in securities, to make decisions to buy or sell financial securities on an exchange.

Algorithmic traders often make use of high-frequency trading technology, which can enable a firm to make tens of thousands of trades per second. No human being can replicate this speed, hence, the software is often replacing human desk traders.

Conventional (manual) trading models only utilize historical data, are often static, require human intervention, and do not perform well when the market changes. Consequently, funds are increasingly migrating towards true AI models that can not only analyse large volumes of data, but also continue to improve themselves.

Most AI trading software today can absorb enormous volumes of data to learn about the world and make predictions about the financial market—stocks, bonds, commodities and other financial instruments. To understand global trends, software can consume everything from books, tweets, news reports, financial data, earnings numbers, and international monetary policy to Saturday Night Live sketches. The AI can keep watching this information all the time, never being tired and always learning and perfecting its predictions.

Let us consider the case of perhaps the most well-known investment banks, Goldman Sachs. In 2014, Goldman Sachs reportedly invested in and began installing an AI-driven trading platform called Kensho. The usage of this gradually increased, as exemplified by this remarkable statistic: In 2000, Goldman Sach's US cash equities trading desk in its New York headquarters employed 600 traders buying and selling stock. Today, it has reportedly just two equity traders, with machines doing the rest.

This has essentially been replicated at a macro scale. After a gradual start, by 2010, upwards of 60 per cent of all trades were executed by computers, with the figure rising over 70 per cent more recently. In India as well, the percentage of trades executed by computers has crossed the 40 per cent mark. Readers may be interested to read Michael Lewis' *Flash Boys* that brought high-frequency, algorithmic trading to the general public's attention, which spoke about the lives of Wall Street traders and entrepreneurs who helped build the companies that came to define the structure of electronic trading in America.

An interesting tenet of his book was that Wall Street firms were engaged in a race to build ever faster computers, which could communicate with exchanges ever more quickly, to gain advantage on competitors solely through speed, thus completely overpowering those who used more traditional methods to trade on the exchange.

Nowadays, even DIY (or do-it-yourself) algorithmic trading has become common. A hedge fund called Quantopian, for instance, crowd source algorithms from amateur program-mers who compete to win commissions for writing the most profitable code.

What is also noteworthy is the potential of these algorithms to get better and better. As most software today rely on machine learning, programs can improve themselves through an iterative process called deep learning.

Why is algorithmic trading popular? Broadly, it provides the following benefits:

- Trades can be executed at the best possible prices.

- Trade order placement is instant and accurate.

- Trades are timed correctly and instantly to avoid significant price changes.

- Reduced transaction costs.

- Simultaneous automated checks on multiple market conditions.

- Reduced risk of manual errors when placing trades.

- Algo-trading can be backtested using available historical and real-time data to see if it is a viable trading strategy.

- Reduced possibility of mistakes by human traders based on emotional and psychological factors.

There are many other benefits of AI based products, some especially relevant for developing nations such as India. In our country, for example, aspects such as the pricing of financial products like insurance policies, the decision to extend credit facilities (including credit cards) suffer in the absence of information about end users due to the absence of credit records and user profiles. As AI and digital technologies become more widespread, some of these issues could be resolved, at least partially.

AI allows for new ways of pricing financial products. A piece of software called Lenddo, for example, can reportedly look at a potential applicants' entire digital footprint to determine their creditworthiness. The company claims that it can look at hundreds of factors including social media account use, internet browsing, geolocation data and other smartphone information.

Their machine learning algorithm turns all this data into a credit score, which banks and other lenders can use towards provision of a credit score; and avoiding the issue of 'adverse selection'. The technology can therefore help extend credit and insurance to those who were hitherto left out of formal channels.

These are all clear compelling benefits that will help the usage of the technology expand in the times to come; not 'features' of the technology. The end result is what matters.

MARKETING DRIVERLESS CARS

The concept of driverless vehicles or 'autonomous cars', as they are also known, is the talk of the town today. I often discuss this in my classes. Generally, the reaction to the concept of self-driving vehicles is mixed, with a number of people feeling that the concept will not work in India for certain country-specific reasons; others raise concerns over the ethical dimensions.

I feel that autonomous cars would suffer from the same issues that the Nano did unless the way they are marketed (especially in India) differs. At the moment, driverless vehicles appear to be promoted as an example of what technology can do and how it has progressed from the days of Henry Ford's Model T.

We are told that the vehicle is 'connected', it has cutting-edge technologies such as LIDAR (Light Detection and Ranging, a device that detects light waves just like the more conventional RADAR detects radio waves), various kinds of sensors, etc. Not many of us would even understand how the technologies work. Therefore, it seems to be a case of expecting consumers to purchase these vehicles for the technology they offer—'technology for technology's sake'.

Instead, autonomous vehicles should be promoted very differently in India. Most results show that such vehicles are involved in far fewer accidents, especially life-threatening crashes, as they eliminate the possibility of human error as well as negligence associated by human being while driving, which could include the usage of a mobile phone while driving, being in an inebriated state, etc.

So, one may wish to market autonomous vehicles on the platform emphasizing that it 'Keeps your Family Safe'. The chances of losing a family member due to a devastating crash could perhaps reduce to a significant extent if your family used an autonomous vehicle. The chance of a parent getting a call that his son or daughter has been involved in a crash on a highway could be much lower. That seems to be a very good reason to buy such a vehicle even if it comes at a premium.

Further, the chance of reduced accidents has a direct bearing on the insurance premium the owner pays. It is quite likely that autonomous vehicles would, therefore, obtain a discount from insurance companies owing to both their likely enhanced safety features preventing theft and/or misuse as well as reduced chance of damages they cause, both to self and to third parties. Hence, the second platform to market autonomous vehicles could be the reduced yearly insurance premium to be paid.

Would you feel as sceptical if you were told that autonomous vehicles:

- Would keep your family safer?
- Would result in your having to pay less for insurance?

It is likely that these considerations would make the average car owner consider driverless cars more favourably. Why? This is because the focus is now on the Benefits that autonomous vehicles bring to the consumer, rather than the features, i.e., the stack of technologies being used.

GETTING IT RIGHT

So how do you make sure that as a marketer you get things right? You could use what is called the 'Features Benefit Matrix' (Table 4.1). This is something I strongly advised my teams or my clients to put in place before they approved any marketing communications or advertisements.

Such a tool helps you to ensure that your messaging is consistent, relevant and impactful. It's simple enough—it has one column for features and a few for the related benefits;

Table 4.1 **FEATURES BENEFIT MATRIX**

S. NO.	FEATURE	BENEFIT 1	BENEFIT 2	BENEFIT 3

along with an additional one at the end for specific messaging data points or calls-to-action.

Using this simple format, you can quickly and easily identify each of the unique benefits offered by your product's features. This, in turn, could help make the process of formulating impactful messaging much more easily.

It also has the very important added benefit of ensuring that all teams, especially both the R&D, sales and marketing and branding teams are on the same page in terms of what is being communicated to end-users and why.

KNIGHT IN SHINING ARMOUR: SELLING BENEFITS

A powerful way in which companies could get the message of the product's benefits across to prospective consumers is through the method of storytelling. In this, the product is usually portrayed as the 'knight in shining armour', while the problem to be solved takes the role of the 'villain'. The product is used to 'save the day' in some form or the other; hence, the benefits of its usage are strongly brought out.

HUL's marketing and promotion of its Fair & Lovely cream indeed uses this method. As I have outlined earlier, the company's advertisement was based on how a woman changed her destiny after using the product. She was not able to get a job or a coveted role in a play, but after she used the product she achieved a different outcome and was successful. The product thus becomes the 'knight in shining armour'; and the consumer is driven towards an emotional connect towards it.

Baba Ramdev of Patanjali fame used a similar approach when he hinted that multinational companies were overcharging

Indian consumers for simple FMCG products such as tooth-pastes and soaps, and that they were made from synthetic ingredients. His products offered an alternative—products 'made in India' that were cheaper and based on natural ingredients.

Products which provide an experience also use this approach. For example, wines may be sold by inviting selected people to tour the vineyards (today people could be taken on a virtual tour using Virtual Reality), thus promoting the authenticity and heritage of the product.

There are many such examples. Subtly promoting benefits through stories strikes an emotional chord with the user, even while he may not realize that his sentiments are being played on.

TESTIMONIALS

Testimonials are yet another way in which brands promote benefits. Look carefully at most testimonials. They, once again, do not speak much about features. Rather, testimonials are almost always about the benefits that the product provides. For example, the testimonial of a cosmetic product may be from an actress stating how her skin looks ever-youthful by using a particular cosmetic. The testimonial of a coaching centre may highlight students who scored well in an exam after taking the classes.

A particular teacher's testimonial may read, 'Mr X helped me grasp a difficult subject easily and solved all my doubts'; hardly ever will you see a testimonial here that reads, 'Mr X has 15 years' experience and has studied management from an IIM'.

In my experience, there are many ways of making testimonials and the storytelling approach outlined above to promote benefits more effective. There are two aspects that I suggest in particular:

- First, the story or testimonial should emphasize what's unique to your product or your firm. Remember that highlighting benefits that are generic to your product or industry may succeed in getting the customer to buy but he may do so from your competitor! For example, highlighting the benefits of a low calorie sweetener could convince the user to purchase such products but, as I said, he may purchase a competitor's sweetener.

  So, stress on benefits that differentiate you from the competition and clearly bring out how you are better. In the above example, you may state that 'Using our product helps you lose weight twice as fast as our competitor's product'.

- Second, the benefits should be seen as concrete; this may mean quantifying them. Stories with many adjectives may sound nice but appear vague and lack credibility. For example, it is better for a testimonial to say, 'Company X's solution helped us reduce costs by 20 per cent', rather than 'Company X's solution helped us to radically reduce costs'.

WHEN MARKETING FEATURES WORK

Of course, there are exceptions to the concept of marketing the benefits rather than the features. Which are these? At times the features may be important to the consumer and he may explicitly want to know about the new features of a new product.

While I have spoken about Steve Jobs' wonderful way of communicating the benefits of Apple's iPod, the company has often highlighted features when it has marketed its iPhone. Every time a new version of the iPhone is launched, users wish to know about the latest features that Apple has incorporated. Apple actively promotes these and makes them part of its marketing strategy (however, it must be pointed out that even Apple struggled when it failed to link explicit benefits with the features as in the case of a recently launched version of its iPhone where people did not take to its new feature of 'wireless charging' which Apple was trying to promote).

Similarly, the trend of marketing using 'product unboxing' also hypes up the features of the device. But then one can always say that the user is given sufficient time in these cases to fully understand and grasp the features and how they can help. One way of looking at this is that when you have a large enough community of 'geeks' who are truly interested in features, it may well make sense to push the features in your communication.

To the geek community, the way in which Apple has continually improved the core specifications of the iPhone to make them increasingly powerful without compromising on Apple's unique design sensibilities is indeed a big deal. Hence, the geeks appreciate the difference between a dual-core 1.4 GHz ARM v8 Typhoon processor that the iPhone 6 uses and the 64-bit A10 Fusion chip with an embedded M10 motion coprocessor that the iPhone 7 has. But laypersons don't really understand all this, do they?

The case of B2B marketing of software products needs to be handled carefully. If you are speaking to IT folks who understand features, you may wish to harp about these.

However, it may not work all the time, hence, it may well be safer to push the benefits even in such cases.

Slack, the popular communications platform, throws up an example of this. The communications platform may offer a range of handy tools and features that streamline team-based communication, but perhaps the real selling point is the time it offers to save. Hence, much of Slack's messaging focuses on how the product can help increase productivity and transparency, a clearly defined benefit-driven approach. At the same time, its features page on its website and marketing collateral also outlines all the things Slack can do.

Many Software as a Service (SaaS) companies use benefits-driven messaging in their campaigns because they realize that buyers don't need their products for their own sake, but because they want to solve specific problems. That's why you'll often see SaaS companies combining feature-driven information with benefits-driven messaging.

YOUR MESSAGING MUST COMMUNICATE THE BENEFITS

Feature-based marketing could work well for certain businesses and product lines. However, in most cases, for large and small businesses, established and new products, across sectors, it is identifying and highlighting how their products and services can improve the lives of their customers which is a much more powerful strategy. Since features rely on communicating facts, they may not emotionally resonate with your customer; and he may not really understand them. For example, the technical specs on a laptop might not make sense to a customer unless he/she is familiar with computers.

The examples of Steve Jobs' messaging for the iPod, Charles Revson's understanding of what sells his cosmetics and Tata's failure with the Nano all point to the fact that if you want your marketing to be as effective as possible, your product and its messaging has to really mean something to your customers and provide them a clear benefit. Speaking in terms of benefits rather than just listing of features, whether it's in writing or in person, means that you're speaking in a language that your customers understand. So dig deep to find and communicate well the benefits you offer!

Chapter 5

Perspective Shift: Solving Problems the Mahatma Way!

Any intelligent fool can make things bigger and more
complex.
It takes a touch of genius—and a lot of courage—to move
in the opposite direction.
—Albert Einstein

EINSTEIN: THE MANAGEMENT GURU OF THE 21ST CENTURY

I always felt that Albert Einstein, one of the greatest physicists that the world has ever seen, a Nobel Prize winner in his chosen field and a true genius (he was only 26 when in 1905, he had four separate papers published, among them his groundbreaking special theory of relativity, as well as his famous equation, $E = mc^2$!) should have been a management professor.

He would perhaps have won as many accolades for his work in management as he did in physics; though he would perhaps have not turned the world on its head as he did with science, by recognizing and quantifying how mass could be converted into energy (which in turn, paved the way for the invention of the atomic bomb) and his work on how gravity affects light. Einstein was named as the Person of the Century by the *Time* magazine in 1999.

Einstein said many things which are equally relevant to management as they were to science. I have shared with my students and audience many of his aphorisms and views which, when applied to the field of business and management, are equally appropriate as they were to science. Have a look at these gems. Some of these were originally said by the great scientist, some were said by others but mentioned effectively by him and a few were not reportedly actually said by him but have been attributed to him (at times incorrectly!):

- 'Everybody is a genius. But if you judge a fish by its ability to climb a tree, it will live its whole life believing that it is stupid.'

- 'Any intelligent fool can make things more complex.... It takes a touch of genius—and a lot of courage to move in the opposite direction.'

- 'Imagination is more important than knowledge. Knowledge can take you from place A to B, but imagination can take you anywhere.'

- 'If you can't explain it simply, you don't understand it well enough.'

- 'Anyone who has never made a mistake has never tried anything new.'

- 'We cannot solve problems with the same thinking that created them.'

- 'Insanity is doing the same thing over and over again and expecting different results.'

- 'In the middle of difficulty lies opportunity.'

- 'It's not that I'm so smart, it's just that I stay with problems longer.'

- 'Education is not the learning of facts, it's rather the training of the mind to think.'

- 'Try not to become a man of success, but rather try to become a man of value.'

All these pithy quotes give an insight into the mind of Einstein. All of the quotes above are equally applicable to anyone in the corporate world, almost across levels. And he got it right almost every time.

I always ask my students to spend some time carefully pondering over the following two quotes mentioned earlier.

- 'We cannot solve problems with the same thinking that created them.'

- 'Insanity is doing the same thing over and over again and expecting different results.'

The year was 1991. The prime minister of India was the enigmatic polyglot Mr P. V. Narasimha Rao and the finance minister, the redoubtable Dr Manmohan Singh (who subsequently himself went on to serve as the prime minister for two terms from 2004 onwards) and India was facing an economic crises. So deep was the issue that the country was left with enough foreign exchange to pay off only two weeks of imports and no other country or major financial institution was willing to lend.

India had to go with the proverbial begging bowl to the International Monetary Fund (IMF), the lender of last resort for help. The IMF asked India to provide 42 ton gold as collateral for its bail-out funding, which had to be airlifted to the Bank of England.

Together with this bail-out, the IMF pushed India into implementing a slew of reforms that collectively came to be called 'Liberalization, Privatization, Globalization' (LPG). These included radical measures such as devaluation of currency (Dr Manmohan Singh devalued the currency by approximately 50 per cent), replacing the policy of import substitution with a focus on increased exports, opening up the economy to foreign investment, abolition the licensing system, etc.

There have been many critics of IMF's policies, most notably Joseph Stiglitz in his book *Globalization and Its Discontents*, but there cannot be much criticism of the IMF's broad philosophy. The IMF always suggests some 'reform' or the other, asking a country to mend its ways. Sometimes the reforms work, sometimes they don't.

Well, they certainly can be said to have worked for India, which soon found itself well on the path to recovery and robust growth. The country's foreign exchange rose over a relatively short period amongst the highest in the world, enough to cover well over a year of imports. Today, India is a net lender to the IMF and is mooting a 'BRICS bank', in which countries such as Brazil, Russia, India, China and South Africa come together to help other developing nations.

What does the IMF really wish to tell the countries who come to it for assistance? Remember, it is the 'lender of last resort', which means countries typically approach the IMF after all other measures to salvage the situation have been tried and come a cropper.

The IMF basically wishes to tell countries (though not perhaps explicitly enough) that they should never forget that their economic policies, their way of managing their own economies had led them to a situation where no one in the world is willing to lend them funds; hence, they had no way but to approach the IMF. If the IMF was to sanction a loan without any pre-condition or without imposing any reform measures, what would have happened?

It is quite likely that the country would soon exhaust the bailout funds and come back to the IMF- with a similar request for more funds. Why? This is because the underlying reasons that cause the crises in the first place have not been addressed.

The country cannot find a solution to its problems with the same thinking that created the issue in the first place. As an example, the thinking could be to promote populism over prudent economic decisions, or have high tax rates, or do the same things again and again and expect different results. It is this thinking that the IMF basically wishes to say, which created the economic crises in the first place. Now the solution cannot lie in the same form of thinking—one has to approach economic issues differently, for which the IMF comes up with some prescriptions.

The author does not claim to be an economist skilled enough to judge the quality of the IMF's interventions or its successes or failures. However, the author wishes to state that he is unequivocally a supporter of the overall approach—if one wishes to achieve different results, one has to do different things or do things differently.

This is exactly what Albert Einstein, my favourite management guru, said. He termed it 'insane' to expect to try doing the same thing again and again and get a different result. One needs to do different things; or do the same thing but in different ways or using different methods.

India's economic history is testimony to the truth of this simple enough aphorism. Having followed a policy of import substitution earlier and keeping the currency overvalued (through a Central Bank determined exchange rate), the rupee was made partially floating (called a 'managed currency system') and devalued to encourage exports achieving quite different results.

While studying economics at Delhi University's Shri Ram College of Commerce (SRCC), I came across the work of noted Indian economists Vijay Joshi and I. M. D. Little. This is what they had to say about the 1991 crises in their seminal study of the Indian economy: the 1991 crisis was a 'policy-induced crisis par excellence'. It had been caused in their opinion, by more than a decade of imprudence. It would only be a radical change in the way of managing the economy that could ensure that it never manifested itself.

MASTERCARD'S 'PRICELESS' STRATEGY

While I was with Hindustan Unilever in 2004, HUL in India was being led by Manvinder Banga. I was surprised to learn that his brother, Ajay Banga, was no less illustrious, but made his name in a slightly different world from FMCG, in that of finance. This was after he had worked with PepsiCo, however, and studied management in the same renowned management institute as his brother, the Indian Institute of Management (IIM Ahmedabad).

Ajay Banga today heads Mastercard, one of the world's well-known firms, as its President and Chief Executive Officer (CEO). It is noteworthy how Ajay Banga has pushed his company into embracing change and innovation, hence, doing things differently.

A Fortune magazine article in 2014[1] spoke about how the then new CEO had led the transformation in his firm. At his first offsite leadership meeting after taking over as president and CEO, he reportedly waxed eloquent with his senior management team about the downside of cash as it was hard to track and could be used for all kinds of illegal activities such as financing drugs, weapons, and tax evasion; also, it was massively expensive to produce (just the cost to produce and distribute it ran the Central bank of an average country up to 1.5 per cent of GDP).

Banga was a man on a mission. When he was asked to head Mastercard in 2010, disrupters such as Square and PayPal were starting to make their presence felt in mobile payments. Mastercard, the company most people associated with a piece of plastic in their pockets, needed to, therefore, go virtual, digital, and biometric. Banga made sure it went the whole hog, experimenting with facial-recognition software, mobile-payment systems, touchless transactions, and its own idea of a 'digital wallet'.

---

[1] Daniel Roberts, 'How MasterCard Became a Tech Company', *Fortune*, 24 July 2014; https://fortune.com/2014/07/24/mastercard-tech-company/, accessed on 24 October 2019.

It is extensively using big data and analytics to give its customers better insight, and even has a special laboratory for experimental new ventures. In short, Banga, with his early experience in FMCG marketing, was leading his company to what could be called Mastercard 2.0.

Banga's company has for long had to compete with larger rival Visa. In many ways, the business was a two-horse, Coke-and-Pepsi-style, with Visa being the larger of the two players. One key issue was that the two brands were more or less interchangeable in consumers' minds, since both are accepted nearly everywhere.

Banga believed that the key to getting consumers to reach for Mastercard instead of Visa lay in developing and offering the consumer technology that makes the purchase experience smoother for both customers and merchants.

While Mastercard's core competency had always been the technology infrastructure that connected its network of more than 25,000 banks to more than 2 billion cards used in over 200 countries across the world, Banga decided to take this to a totally new level. He launched an in-house innovation arm, Mastercard Labs, in 2010 when he was still COO. PayPass, its contactless technology, was rolled out in 2012.

Masterpass, the company's digital wallet (it stores your personal data to more quickly complete a purchase from any device, using any brand of card) followed, in February 2013. One product that Mastercard Labs came up with was 'Shop This!' which let customers purchase items from within a magazine App. They could click on an advertisement for a men's cologne, for example, and buy it right there.

Then there was 'in Control', which let Mastercard users carry just one Card but set it to charge either one's credit or debit account for purchases above or below an amount that he/she chose. It could also work in a manner to parental controls on a television set, restricting the type of store where the card could be used.

Banga's ideas around digital wallets allowed Mastercard to partner in Lebanon and Jordan with the UN World Food Programme to give Syrian refugees Mastercards loaded with $27 per week for food. In political crisis zones such as Russia and Egypt, many government employees were given their salaries on prepaid Mastercards. In case there is a crisis and banking systems are rendered frozen, their cards will still be refilled automatically.

There are many other examples of companies doing things differently to get different results, especially results that are beyond the usual. Companies such as Google, Apple, Amazon and so on pride themselves on their ability to come up with innovative products. What makes this possible? Enough and more has been written about the different 'work culture' at the offices of these firms that foster a spirit of curiosity and innovation.

Some of the perks that make Google an extremely employee-friendly and productive workspace include chef-prepared meals, nap pods where employees can take a quick forty winks and rejuvenate themselves, play video games, provision of free health and dental care, subsidies for buying hybrid cars, employee trips, gyms, financial bonuses and more.

Frederik Pferdt, head of innovation and creativity programs at Google in 2016, explained that a typical Google office actually tries to encourage employees to rediscover the child within by being curious and asking questions, stating that normally a human being's creativity wanes as he ages. Hence, Google tries to recreate a children's playground with its offices to awaken their employee's wild imagination, similar to that of a young child, who does not have typical mental constraints or the cynicism associated with older adults; it is only in such an environment that people can think of what is seemingly impossible such as driverless cars. 'What is happening in most organizations is that people lose the ability to not just come up with ideas, but the courage to share those ideas with each other with pride,' Pferdt said. 'We are trying to establish an environment where people can share ideas which might not be finished, might not be perfect, but are attempts to start disrupting things, to start a discussion of things that may be impossible at the moment.'[2]

Similarly, companies that have disrupted the world of business have also succeeded in doing so through doing things differently. Be it an Uber or an AirBnB or an Amazon, these firms have shaken up traditional sectors such as transportation, hospitality and retail, respectively, through their different models.

While Amazon is a 'virtual market place' offering a platform where buyers and sellers can be put in touch, companies such as Uber and AirBnB have shaken the world by owning no assets whatsoever and still becoming the largest in their sectors, which traditionally relied on companies owning or having access to as many properties (movable in one case and immovable in the other) than their competitors.

In fact, Alibaba has taken the concept of a marketplace connecting buyers and sellers to a whole new level, owning no inventory at all. In fact, it serves a larger 'national' purpose since most of the sellers on its platform are Chinese, who are connected with buyers around the world. The value that

---

[2] Marlet D. Salazar, 'Google's Culture of Innovation', *Inquirer*, November 2016 https://technology. inquirer.net/55507/googles-culture-of-innovation#ixzz5vCJ0WO9W, accessed on 24 October 2019.

Alibaba provides, lies almost purely in the software interface and concomitant technologies (including data about its customers), not in the products sold on the platform.

Another example of different thinking that led to success was Google Maps, today a ubiquitous App that nearly everyone uses. Google used the idea of almost literally 'crowdsourcing innovation' to improve the quality of its Google Maps. The idea apparently emerged when one of Google's engineering teams in India realized that the lack of online map data would limit the usefulness of Google Maps in India and other developing nations.

Rather than trying to get the data themselves, they decided to create a platform wherein users could provide the missing data. This idea led to Google Map Maker, a tool that lets anyone make changes to Google Maps. Today, thousands of citizen cartographers around the world are literally making the product more accurate and reliable.

A company in the more traditional space that thought very differently from its peers was JC Decaux. Its street furniture is almost ubiquitous in many major cities of the world, including in New Delhi. What is remarkable about this street furniture is that it has all been provided free by the French company to the respective municipalities!

YOUNG MAN, BIG IDEA

The company is named after its founder, Jean-Claude Decaux, who was born into a modest family of shoe-shop owners in 1937. The young Jean-Claude was a strong believer of advertising influencing sales and decided to display advertising posters in the early 1950s for the family shop in the city. This initiative, which was not common at the time, gained him recognition. He became a poster sticker for other retailers in the city of Beauvais, France, where Decaux was based.

Jean-Claude soon decided set up his own billboard company, while still in his teens. He was moderately successful, but the French Finance Act 1964 planned to impose higher taxes on roadside advertising displays in order to reduce their number in the countryside. The still young Jean-Claude had to clearly think differently. And this he did by devising the radical plan which he pitched to various city mayors: providing and maintaining bus shelters, financed by advertising. The Municipalities would not need to pay anything.

The Mayor of Lyon was the first to adopt this idea, in 1964. The advertising-based bus shelter and the Decaux business model were thus born; and the young Jean-Claude Decaux had revolutionized outdoor advertising. At last count, the company, with its humble beginnings, is today present in over 60 countries.

THINK DIFFERENT

So having said that one needs to do different things or do things differently if one wants to achieve different results, how does one begin to do this? Clearly, it involves thinking on different lines, and this is easier said than done; for it involves changing one's established and time-tested way of doing things.

Indeed, the more experience one has, the more difficult it is to change the way one thinks or approaches tasks. After all, we have all reached where we are owing to our current thought processes and ways of doing things. Now adopting new ways is clearly not easy as one tends to follow the patterns of thought and action that we have long established for ourselves and indeed, come to rely on.

PARADIGM SHIFTS

According to the *Stanford Encyclopedia of Philosophy*, Thomas Samuel Kuhn (1922–1996) was one of the most influential philosophers of science in the 20th century. His book titled *The Structure of Scientific Revolutions* (1962) is one of the most cited academic books of all time.

What does Thomas Kuhn have to say and what is its relevance to management?

Kuhn described a simple cycle of scientific progress called the 'Kuhn Cycle' in *The Structure of Scientific Revolutions*, challenging the world's conception of science that related to a steady progression of the accumulation of new ideas. By studying past major scientific advances, Kuhn showed that this view was inaccurate and that science had actually advanced not by small incremental steps, but by occasional revolutionary explosions of new knowledge.

Each of these revolutions was triggered by the introduction of new ways of thought so different from the earlier ones, that they could be called new paradigms. In fact, it was from Kuhn's 1962 work that we get the popular use of terms such as 'paradigm', 'paradigm shift' and 'paradigm change'.

What is worth noting is that paradigm shifts were all caused by new ways of thinking and looking at existing problems or issues. Very often, these new ways of thinking were the result of crises, in the sense that the old paradigms could no longer account for scientifically observed phenomena, thus, the current theories were wrong or clearly needed some modification.

A paradigm could be said to be a comprehensive model of understanding that provides a discipline's members with viewpoints, guidelines and rules on how to look at that field's problems and how to solve them. Accordingly, a 'paradigm shift' could be termed as an important change that happens when the usual way of thinking about or doing something is replaced by a new and different way.

Often when we confront a management problem, it is clear that a 'paradigm shift', i.e., a new way of thinking is needed. Einstein meant this when he said that solutions to problems could not be found by using the same thinking that created the problem in the first place. As we discussed from the IMF example, the multilateral institution expects countries to also make such 'paradigm shifts' in the way they manage their country.

CHANGING OUR PERCEPTIONS AND PARADIGMS

The crux, therefore, is for us, as individuals, when confronted with seemingly insurmountable problems, to try and radically change the way we look at things. This may be done, of course, after we have exhausted our tried and tested techniques, and still failed to get the results we want.

For example, a company faced with declining sales may have already tried the usual strategies of changing pricing or other measures it has resorted to in the past; and similarly, companies faced with high attrition may first try the usual techniques of changing incentive structures, etc., without making much impact.

Let us consider a situation. There is a party going on and everyone is dancing on the dance floor. You too are enjoying the dance with your partner; but take a moment, while dancing to look around you. You may notice a few things; but you may also miss a few, given that you are very much in the dance.

On the other hand, there is a person watching the dance from a balcony above. He is not part of the dance but just an observer. The view he gets and the observations he makes may be very different from the person who is 'in the dance'. The 'balcony view' and that of a person 'in the dance' are actually different paradigms.

Sometimes, therefore, even as you are in the dance, it may help to take the view of the external observer. Executives of all kinds, be they junior or senior, who are chasing daily targets and worried about monthly numbers sometimes may wish to ask someone who is in the balcony. This 'balcony' perspective could come from an external consultant or someone from a different function or department or even one's friend or spouse.

Very often it will be different from the views and opinion of those 'in the dance'.

An important skill for any executive to have is the ability to sometimes change his own perspective. As outlined earlier, he may seek the views of an external person for this. But better still, he can coach himself to develop an ability to find new perspectives himself, without asking others.

Consider the captain in a cricket match. He has to make many decisions on the field, while he is 'in the dance'. It is not feasible for him to ask external observers or the team coach who maybe observing from the balcony and taking the 'balcony view' for advice. He has to be both 'in the dance' as well as be able to 'take the balcony view' himself.

So is the case with corporate executives often, for indeed, only they understand the context and have a full understanding of the problems and issues in front of them. One can engage an external consultant or consultancy firm, but this involves cost, cannot be done always and cannot be expected to result in quick solutions for the consultant also needs time to grasp matters. Decision makers in the corporate sector, therefore, have often to make decisions themselves (of course with their team) and they could always benefit from a healthy dose of being able to undertake a 'paradigm shift'.

How does one change his perspective/paradigm?

YOUR GRANDMOTHER AND MR TRUMP

So how does one change his perspectives or way of thinking? While there may be many possibilities, I have found one technique to be particularly useful.

This technique involves asking oneself a series of related questions, with the objective of prodding one's brain to break with its existing paradigms, or perspectives, and develop a new lens with which to approach the matter.

These series of questions are as follows. Ask yourself:

- How would Mahatma Gandhi solve this matter?
- How would Bill Gates approach this issue (or any other corporate honcho you may have admired)?
- How would Donald Trump manage this problem?
- How would the current prime minister of India manage this issue? How would the previous prime minister do it?
- How would a six-year-old boy or girl try and deal with this issue?
- If you approached your grandmother, what would she have to advise regarding this matter?

And so on. You can keep putting different people and extending the list of questions. What are we doing here?

We are recognizing that Trump or your grandmother or your six-year-old son or daughter represent different paradigms and have different perspectives, different ways of thinking and doing things. The approaches can be looked at to solve an issue. There is no compulsion to rely on your own technique. You can tap into others' techniques as well.

For example, if you are faced with two small children getting into a fight, how does a child solve the matter? He may give his adversary a punch or alternately he may go running to complain to his elder brother or parent, asking them to intervene. But how would a grandmother act? She would likely try to mollify both parties and get the two kids to play again.

The point here being that there are always multiple ways of addressing any issue—have you considered all of them? Mostly we don't, relying only on our own paradigms.

MUNNA BHAI MBBS

I once had the opportunity to engage with a company which published a major daily newspaper that had one of the highest circulations in the country. They were faced with stagnant sales and had tried various usual strategies—changing the price, adding more pages, more supplements, etc., but all this had had little impact.

This company's executives went into a huddle and adopted the technique outlined above. They asked themselves, 'What would Mahatma Gandhi do if he were running the management of this publication?'

In the immensely successful sequel to the movie *Munna Bhai MBBS*, called *Lage Raho Munna Bhai* (a 2006 Indian comedy-drama film directed by Rajkumar Hirani and produced by

Vidhu Vinod Chopra), the character played by Sanjay Dutt starts to see the spirit of Mahatma Gandhi. He begins to hallucinate that the Father of the Nation is advising him on what he should do next and uses the technique of 'Gandhigiri' to help ordinary people solve their problems.

The executives of this publication also studied and understood how the Mahatma solved major issues. He associated with causes that he saw as important and aimed to influence the way these panned out. For the Mahatma, these causes included the freedom of India, as well as boycotting foreign cloth, Hindu–Muslim unity, ensuring that women and the oppressed castes got their due, people followed the principle of non-violence, etc.

It was this whole-hearted devotion to causes that made the Mahatma a mass leader and ensured he captured the public imagination (indeed, this theme of leaders being devoted to causes much bigger than immediate needs runs consistently through the study of great leaders, be it Abraham Lincoln who took a stand against slavery or even a Christ or a Buddha).

The executives accordingly decided that they would ensure that their publication too associates with important 'causes' and issues that confronted the nation at any point in time; promoting these extensively in their advertisements and giving such causes plenty of visibility in their publication. Some of these themes the publication chose to associate with included the 'Teach India' campaign, 'Read India', etc.

This different strategy, gleaned from changing existing paradigms (that usually included changes in pricing, editorial content, etc.) helped the publication achieve very different results from what it would have done had it continued with its usual strategies or tactics.

There is clearly much to be gained by trying out new things, doing things differently and taking the occasional risk and this can only be done by changing one's style or thought processes or ways of action. When faced with challenges that seem intractable, it is often these techniques that bring the best results. Einstein was absolutely spot-on when he observed that different results cannot be achieved through the repetition of past actions; it is only new ways of thought and action that result in breakthroughs.

Consider the example of fitness. The manner in which a child looks at the concept of fitness will be very different from that of a middle-aged adult, and from that of a more aged one. A child may relate fitness, not to exercise but to fun and play. A company in the business of fitness, could therefore, consider putting in the fun element into its offerings. How could it make its solutions resemble play more than exercises?

Such changes born out of 'perspective shifts' also gives you a head-start over competition, as these moves are often unexpected. Competition may well be prepared for a price-war or other similar competitive moves, but a radically different approach catches them off-guard. If they respond in the like manner, they risk being seen as a follower, rather than the industry trend-setter.

Chapter 6

The Strategic Thinking and Problem-Solving Mindset

There is nothing so useless as doing efficiently that which should not be done at all.

—Peter Drucker

The word 'strategy' has always meant different things to different people; and has often been misused. It indeed has been fashionable for long to add the word 'strategic' to almost anything, be it any kind of work, function or discipline.

Thus, many companies claim to advance 'strategic marketing', 'strategic brand building', 'strategic HR', 'strategic planning' and the like.

So what exactly constitutes strategy and what are the skills that someone who wishes to excel in this domain should possess? This is an important question, for I have seen that most executives both lack an understanding of what constitutes strategy and the skills to ensure that they get strategies right.

Very many executives, however, are good at tactical plays; which works till the time that their business faces a major disruption. The problem is that the number and extent of disruptions are increasing today, catching many off guard and resulting in many companies realizing, too late, that they have not really been good at strategy, but only at tactical ploys.

WHAT IS STRATEGY?

Kenichi Ohmae has been called 'Mr Strategy' across the world and according to the *Financial Times* of London, he is 'Japan's only management guru'. In 1994, *The Economist* selected him as one of the five management gurus in the world.

Ohmae was born in 1943 in Japan during the Second World War and earned an MS in nuclear physics in 1968 from the Tokyo Institute of Technology, and later a doctorate in nuclear engineering from the Massachusetts Institute of Technology in 1970.

From 1972 to 1995 he worked for McKinsey & Company; where as a senior partner, he ran the company's Japan operations for a number of years, co-founding its strategic management practice, and advising companies in a wide spectrum of industries, including industrial and consumer electronics, finance, telecommunications, food and chemicals.

Ohmae introduced the Japanese management methods to a broad Western audience, specifically the Toyota practice of just-in-time production.

Kenichi Ohmae had perhaps the best definition, if there could be one, of what strategy is. More than anyone else, he effectively distinguished strategy from undertaking measures that increase in better efficiency, cost reduction or mere changes in productivity.

His concept of strategy includes the following salient points:

- True strategy are those set of actions that are aimed at directly altering the strength of a company relative to that of its competitors

- When one is striving to maintain a position of relative superiority over a competitor, the mindset has to be very different than when the objective is to make internal improvements to be more efficient—it is the 'difference between going to battle and going on a diet'

This blue-blooded guru of strategy was remarkably eloquent. According to him, there are clearly two objectives that companies look at:

- Competing in the marketplace by doing something better than all others, i.e., having a source of competitive advantage and maintaining it.

- Setting benchmarks by comparing oneself to peers and being the best in class with respect to those parameters—in terms of efficiency, productivity, etc.

What Kenichi Ohmae wished to say was that the first constituted true strategic actions. Everyday companies compete with their peers, going into a battle as it were for market share and share of the consumer's mind or wallet. Strategic initiatives are designed to keep one's company ahead of one's competitors, superior in some terms, be it in quality, service, innovations or any such action, but one needs to obtain and maintain a position of relative superiority in the battle. A failure to maintain superiority in a battle could mean death for an individual, and likewise for a company.

The second aspect was companies just wishing to look good, as does someone who goes on a diet. This was, therefore, not about survival, it was more about establishing internal benchmarks to strive towards and derive a sense of satisfaction if those benchmarks were achieved. Here the pressure and motivation was completely different.

Kenichi Ohmae was fairly accurate in distinguishing between the two. In a disruptive world, only those companies which successfully maintain a relative superiority over their competitors (and the nature and type of competitors is always broadening) have delivered stellar returns to their shareholders and created value in the long run.

Those who, on the other hand, have been on a 'diet' as Ohmae puts it, have seen their business being disrupted; a radical change in the industry has meant that some kind of technology has come in that has changed the rules of the game and made the internal improvements on the parameter of efficiency redundant.

When considering costs as well, one can choose to be 'strategic' or merely tactical. Ohmae, as earlier mentioned, was credited with having introduced Japanese concepts such as Toyota's 'Just-in-time' production system to Western audiences. This was an example of strategically targeting costs by changing the cost structure itself, thus giving the firm in question a look of 'relative superiority'. Other such tools that could provide relative superiority with respect to costs were choice of commodities or raw materials; and the use of automation. Another option could be to combine certain key functions with other businesses, sharing overhead costs, examples could be transport, warehousing or call centres. On the other hand, trying to squeeze one's supplier by bargaining harder was an example of a tactical measure, akin to going on a diet (or making the supplier going on a diet, in this case).

Think of the automotive industry. While the traditional automotive firms have been making ever efficient automobile engines, hence 'dieting' fairly efficiently; their very survival is being threatened by new technologies such as electric vehicles or driverless cars (which also run on batteries). To maintain their position, let alone superiority, the traditional firms have had to look at their business with a completely new perspective, rather than make further improvements in efficiency alone (by 'dieting' some more).

How the market saw these developments was best reflected in the fact that at one time, the market capitalization of battery specialist Tesla was more than that of the three largest US automakers (General Motors, Ford and Chrysler) combined.

Ohmae was also very accurate when he stated that the mindset of people going into battle and fighting to stay alive, needed to be totally different from those who were just trying to look good (by going on a diet). It was only those with the former mindset who could be called strategic thinkers.

I have worked for long in the energy industry and have noticed that one Indian company which has been good with its strategic thinking has been India's most profitable firm—Reliance Industries Ltd (RIL). They have generally looked to disrupt the market with measures that provide their firm with a clear competitive advantage—the relative superiority over their competitors that Kenichi Ohmae spoke about.

In the case of the refining and petrochemical segment plant, they achieved this 'relative superiority' by building refineries which incorporated the following characteristics:

- Much higher complexity in terms of the 'Nelson complexity index' than their competitors which allowed the refinery to process heavier, sourer crudes than anyone else. This allowed RIL's Jamnagar refinery to consistently record margins well above Singapore benchmark indices and those of its competitors, especially the Public Sector Undertaking (PSU) refineries owned by Indian Oil Corp (IOC), Bharat Petroleum Corp Ltd (BPCL) and Hindustan Petroleum Corp Ltd (HPCL).

- Achieve considerable economies of scale by ensuring that the refineries had much higher capacity and capacity utilization than their counterparts. The Jamnagar complex boasts two refineries of about 60 million ton per annum capacity, which was much higher than those of other refineries in India at the time of completion. Economies of scale have benefited Chinese companies in many sectors as well.

- Achieving advantages due to the strategic sitting of the refinery on the Gujarat coast, which was relatively close to the potential sources of crude oil and had access to an all-weather port. In comparison, some of the other refineries in India were inland, considerably increasing logistics costs.

- Investing massively in technology, including ensuring that the Jamnagar refinery was perhaps the only one in India to produce zero Fuel Oil (FO) and further increasing margins through projects like commissioning the world's first ever and largest Refinery Off-Gas Cracker (ROGC) complex of 1.5 million metric ton (mmtpa) and a petroleum coke gasification unit said to cost USD 4 billion which further provided a sustainable cost advantage over global peers.

Reliance Industries Ltd has strived to maintain its advantage in other sectors such as telecom as well, where it has again used technology and scale to its advantage, being able to translate this into considerable price advantages in the market.

In my opinion, the set of skills required to deliver on such strategic initiatives so as to obtain an advantage in the market includes the following:

- Ability to possess visionary thinking that includes long-term orientation and to understand trends.

- A very strong analytical ability that leads to genuine good decision-making.

- Creative or 'innovative' mindset that includes the ability to think differently, take the occasional risk (backed up through strong analysis) and put succinctly, do new things or find new solutions to extant issues and problems.

While not all of us are in positions where we can serve as the quintessential visionary leader, it is very much a strong analytical ability coupled with a creative mindset that can help us achieve success and larger profits for our firm.

For it is that firm which understands its customers better (owing often to high quality analysis that leads to opportunity for cross-selling, for example) or finds new and innovative solutions to customers' needs (think the Sony Walkman for instance) that earns superior profits.

Other examples of how quality analysis helps include the following:

- Segmentation of objectives including the use of products and customers (by geography, age, social interests) relevant to cross-selling and other such initiatives.

- Understanding profit sources. Where does the company get most of its profits? Is it through selling existing products, or new products, or by selling services related to products? Often, you will find that the Pareto rule, which states that approximately 80 per cent profits come from approximately 20 per cent products or 20 per cent customers provide close to 80 per cent of the profits applies here. So companies can look to optimize effectively.

- Using analysis to understand the cost structure, especially the difference in the ratio between fixed and variable costs, which can be particularly important to low-turnover companies.

ARE YOU ANCHORED? THE $5 AND $0 CHALLENGE

We have established the importance of one's mindset towards making incremental changes that are tactical in nature or towards genuine strategy and problem-solving. So how can one work towards developing a mindset that is suitable towards strategy and innovation.

First, it is crucial to keep an open mind, encumbered by as few things as possible and be ready to grasp opportunities that come one's way. This is best illustrated by the following research done by a professor. He divided his students into two groups.

The first group was told that they have USD 5 with them and to use this to earn as much as possible in a period of say, four weeks. The second group was told they have USD 0 and told to earn as much as they could with it in the same time period. The group that could earn more would be the winner. Can you guess who won this challenge?

Counter-intuitively, it was the Group with USD 0. The maximum that the group with USD 5 could do was to earn USD 12, which was no mean feat for it meant they had more than doubled their initial funds. Anyone would tell you that their Return on Investment (ROI) was nothing to be sneezed at. However, the group that had nothing (USD 0) to start off with actually ended up with no less than USD 100!

How did they do this?

In this example, they booked a reservation at a table in a much sought after restaurant. As reservations for a particular date were then available, they did not have to pay at the time for the booking. But the reservations gradually began to fill up for that day, and the group was able to re-sell the reservation to a party that was very keen on it for USD 100.

How did this group manage so much better?

One can always say that they had a smarter set of individuals, but I feel there was something else significantly different. The group that had USD 5 was anchored to this amount. They looked at all possibilities as to what they could do with this particular amount. They could invest in the stock of a particular company, for example, and hope that it delivered stellar returns in the given period. Or they could risk it by betting at the races or play roulette poker with it at a casino, hoping to hit the jackpot. Or, they could be more conservative, earning a smaller, but solid return.

In any event, a return of USD 12 on the USD 5 was not bad, but it was much less than what the other group with USD 0 got. What mattered was that their mindset was anchored to the USD 5 and what all could be done with that amount. This meant that they failed to consider many possibilities, for there is only so much that can be done with USD 5.

The other group, on the other hand, had no anchor. This meant that their consideration set was much wider. They considered many more possibilities. They realized there are many more ways of earning money, especially with some time on their hands. They perforce had to have a more open mind- for they started off with what was seemingly a weaker situation. And they won.

How often do we see this manifest itself? Many individuals and companies are anchored by what they have done in the past. A student is anchored by the course he studied in graduation, for example, whereas in reality he can choose to make a career in many more fields than that based on the course he studied.

A company, likewise, need not consider its history or the products it has made when contemplating what it should do in future. The realm of possibilities in reality, is much wider than what it may feel if it remains anchored in the past.

A company from Jaipur, India, where I had the opportunity to work, traditionally used to make electrical transformers. However, the next generation of the company's promoters chose to focus on developing a new business line in AI and Augmented Reality. This company did not allow its past to totally determine its future.

I do not mean to state that companies should diversify into totally unrelated areas forgetting their strengths and core competencies. However, I do mean to advocate that keeping an open mind and grasping opportunities that seem relevant is important.

GOOGLE'S 'THINK 10X'

The Google website[1] states that 'the notion of "10x thinking" is at the heart of how we innovate at Google'. They say that major breakthroughs are the result of a mindset in which people are trying to improve something by 10 times rather than by 10 per cent. Google provides examples such as their major technological advances, including glucose-monitoring contact lenses, balloons that deliver Internet access to remote areas of the world, to self-driving cars.

Google's website goes on to say, 'A 10x goal forces you to rethink an idea entirely. It pushes you beyond existing models and forces you to totally re-imagine how to approach it.'

---

[1] https://gsuite.google.co.in/intl/en_in/learn-more/creating_a_culture_of_innovation.html, accessed on 24 October 2019.

'Blue Sky thinking' or the 'Blue Ocean Strategy' are other such tools that can generate ideas to deliver 10x results. An initiative that I have found particularly useful in the context of setting such goals is for a company to go to a visionary thinker or consultant who is not an employee, but can provide the kind of perspective that an insider cannot. An outsider, if a visionary, can often envision a greater range of possibilities for they are not anchored by the existing ways of doing things.

Better still, an effective way of tapping outsiders is to try and understand what questions an outsider may ask if confronted with an issue. This often helps one to refine his/her own thinking and drive down to the crux of an issue.

For example, Google states that they asked themselves the question: 'What if it could be easier and safer for everyone to get around?' For this to happen to a 10x extent, it was clear that one needed to eliminate one of the primary causes of accidents—human error. So, why not think of cars which will not need human beings to move from one place to another!

CEO Speak: The Story of SPAR in India

SPAR Hypermarkets in India is a result of a partnership between the Dubai-based Landmark Group's Max Hypermarkets India Pvt. Ltd. & the Netherlands based SPAR International. The parent company's history goes back to 1932 and it now has over 12,500 stores in 44 countries; while SPAR India has 24 stores across 9 cities that include Bengaluru, Mangalore, Shimoga, Chennai, Coimbatore, Hyderabad, New Delhi, Gurugram and Ghaziabad.

The company's vision has been simple. It states that it wishes 'to be the most engaging and innovative hypermarket in

India, making a difference in the lives of teams, customers, communities and shareholders, Everyday!'

What is noteworthy is the approach that the brand has adopted in India. Considering a city such as Bengaluru, the company realized that customers were not walking into hypermarkets because of the logistical challenges involved. One had to find space and pay to park one's vehicle and then jostle through crowds while shopping; finally ending up having to wait in long queues at the check-in counter.

Senior executives decided that the way forward was to get close to the customer and provide him a different experience. Shopping should be convenient and fun. Hence, the store layout should allow for easy walkthroughs, while providing the kind of deep assortment the customer wanted and provide him/her the kind of convenience that made for a great shopping experience.

There were, hence, many innovations that the company introduced:

Its website states that it 'believes in offering the freshest of fruits, vegetables, fish, and meat & poultry products, sourced locally or imported, for all our customers'. To ensure this, it introduced a 'Farmers' Market' section where local produce is procured directly from the farmers and transported to SPAR collection centres; where in turn the products are graded and delivered to all the SPAR stores in a city within a short span of time, ensuring freshness. They also introduced a section called 'Freshly' which provides value-added services in the form of fresh fruit juices, salads, and other food items which are freshly made for them.

Next was the dimension of convenience. The company used digital food kiosks that used an interactive interface to provide customers with various recipes with a simple click. The platform lists essential ingredients and required measurements so that the customer can get a more focused shopping experience. The self-assist kiosks have an in-built call facility that enables the customer to reach the nearest store attendant if he or she wishes; with these kiosks being available at various points in the store which helps the customer to locate the exact aisle and shelf, thereby cutting down the idle store time.

The pricing labels were also digitized—the shelf edge labels were designed to display live price updates without any manual intervention. The digital kiosks were coupled with the use of 'SPAR studio' in the home furnishings section; also, a digital touch screen kiosk which serves as a virtual showroom enabling customers to mix and match the colours, shades and patterns to suit their home interiors.

To address the issue of long queues at check-out points, especially on weekends or other holidays, the company developed a 'Q Buster' solution involving self-checkout kiosks; customers could themselves scan the items and pay for them without having to wait in the queues.

Another challenge was to reach the end consumer. Not everyone would travel frequently to a hypermarket located a fair distance from their houses. So SPAR decided that they would reach the consumer themselves instead. They chose to try and 'organize the unorganized sector', in their words, by collaborating with push-cart vendors in various localities to introduce 'SPAR on Wheels'. This project follows a 'Click & Collect' business model in which fresh fruits and vegetables would be delivered through the customers' doorstep if they ordered online.

All these measures have resulted in vastly different results than traditional means could have achieved- and much recognition for the company. SPAR India won at Customer Loyalty Awards 2019 under the category 'Best use of Customer and Data Analytics in Loyalty Program', at the ETCIO Annual Awards 2019 under the category Enterprise Technology, the 'Brand Of The Year Award 2018', by WCRC International (a global brand equity management and consulting firm), the 'Most Admired Omni-Channel Retailer of the Year' award by The IMAGES Retail Tech Awards 2018, etc. I spoke to Rajeev Krishnan, the Managing Director & CEO, Max Hypermarket India Pvt. Ltd (SPAR India) on SPAR's journey. Rajeev has over three decades of global retail and consumer experiences, in the US and India, having worked with Target, Wal-Mart, McKinsey & now SPAR. He was recognized as one of India's 'Most Trusted CEOs' in 2018 by the World Consulting & Research Corporation (WCRC) Asia; and felicitated as 'India's Inspirational Leader 2018–2019' in London under the third edition of Global Indian Excellence Summit.

Rajeev stresses immensely on the need for thinking and doing things differently, saying 'If you keep doing what you have been doing…you will get what you got…. If we keep repeating average or bad performance the output will be the same. It is important to periodically step back, assess, and realign if necessary.' He goes on to say that 'It is important to be aware of what is around you and ensure continuous learning. The moment learning stops…innovation is history!! Be careful of arrogance and the intellectual assumption that we have arrived.'

I spoke to him about the motivations behind some of SPAR's innovative formats in the stores. Rajeev was clear that one needs to keep one's ear to the ground and the customer at the centre of whatever was being done, going on to say, 'Most of the great ideas were a creation of a couple of simple thoughts right in front of us. Don't ignore the obvious as that is what causes the biggest customer pain points…. Innovation needs to be with a free heart and mind and clarity as to who it is for. Be passionate about it and collaborate wherever required.'

When recounting the challenges he faced while implementing the new strategy and innovative formats, Rajeev states, 'The speed with which the change and challenges were overcome were the fastest I had ever experienced in my entire career and working lifetime. Within just 90 days, changes had started, that involved many people in the organization, collaboration with internal and external partners, innovation across functions, and of course, having fun in the office. The key to our success in implementation was that I was able to meet every single team member in the organization within each functional group. We shared, talked discussed and opened up about who we were, where we wanted to go and how. We were all focused on ensuring that all of us would move together and win or lose together.'

He continues, 'There was resistance from a few senior leaders and we had to take decisions where we agreed to disagree, but move. We committed to two critical groups of people in everything we did…our Customers/Guests and our Communities. The emotional quotient was at the core of the whole journey. The other challenge was teams not believing things could be done and or not believing that they could be done at the speed required. But at each stage a group of people with a little coaxing achieved success, and then it spread like wildfire.'

He ends by advising, 'Take the paths less taken as the opportunities too will be more. Embrace risk taking and learn with each jolt. The faster you learn the better the next phase normally is.'

IDEATION TECHNIQUES

There are many techniques that could help you get ideas. Unlike the 10x changes, as outlined earlier, not all of these are intended to produce breakthrough results; nor is it necessary to always strive for a breakthrough. Often small changes, well implemented, are also important, and this is where various ideation techniques come in.

As I have mentioned earlier, the mindset is very important and these techniques help you to build the right mindset of ideation, problem-solving or innovation. This is because a person ideates by combining his/her conscious and unconscious mind, his/her rational thoughts with his/her imagination.

One popular technique devised by Edward de Bono is that of the six thinking hats, where one learns to look at issues through different lens. There is much easily available literature on this, so I will not go into details in this book.

Another technique that I have often used and asked others to try is what is called 'SCAMPER'. I advocate this technique because it is easy for anyone to implement, even for entry-level employees or those at the start of their careers. The six thinking hats involves a person to have a certain level of maturity, changing his mindset depending on the 'hat' he is wearing, but is more useful when used by senior management. SCAMPER, however, works equally well at all levels. What is this technique?

The technique refers to a series of thought creators or provocations which help you innovate on an existing product, service or situation, based on asking a number of simple, easy questions. It is virtually guaranteed to result in generating many possibilities, especially through brainstorming sessions or by working in a team. Hence, the sense of despondency that arises when sales diminish can be evaded and people can feel energized through the exercise as they collectively realize there is still a lot that can be done.

SCAMPER is actually an acronym, standing for the following:

- Substitute
- Combine
- Adapt
- Modify
- Put to another use
- Eliminate
- Reverse

Each of these aspects uses a set of questions that pushes or provokes new thoughts. Take your product or service and ask yourself the following questions (you can add many more questions if you wish); the more the 'thought provokers', the better:

Substitute

- What can I substitute in my product or service so as to make an improvement?
- How can I substitute the place, time, materials or people?
- Can I substitute one part for another or change any part?
- Can I change the fundamentals, i.e., the way people consume my product or service or the way they use it?

- Should I change the name?
- Can I use other ingredients or materials?
- Can I use other processes or procedures?
- Can I use this idea for other projects?

Combine

- What ideas, materials, features, processes, people, products, or components can I combine?
- What can I combine in order to optimize the costs?
- Where can I build synergy?

Adapt

- Which ideas can I adapt, copy, or borrow from other people's products?
- What processes should I adapt?
- Can I adapt my product or service using different technologies?

Modify

- What can I magnify or make larger?
- What can I reduce or even remove from my product?
- Can I modify the target group?
- What can be made higher, bigger or stronger?
- Can I increase its speed or frequency?
- How can I add extra features/value?

Put to Another Use

- What else can my product or service be used for?

- How would a child or a senior citizen use it?

- Which other target group can benefit from this product?

- Would there be other possible uses if I were to modify the product?

Eliminate

- What can I remove without altering its function?

- Can I reduce time or components?

- Can I cut costs by eliminating something?

- How can I simplify it? What is non-essential or unnecessary?

Re-arrange

- What can I rearrange in some way—can I interchange components, the pattern, or the layout?

- Can I change the pace or schedule?

Let us consider using this technique for a restaurant chain. Suppose the executives of this chain were to get together and come up with possibilities. Their ideas could include any or all of the following (this is merely illustrative and you can come up with many more. I strongly suggest you do this for your product or service):

- Put to other uses: Selling restaurants and real estate instead of just simply the food.

- Or creating a franchisee business by franchising out the brand once you have reached a certain number of restaurants on your own and have an established brand

- Eliminate: Letting customers serve themselves and thereby avoiding the use of expensive waiters.

- Eliminate: Using machines to dispense coffee or soft drinks thereby eliminating the need of manual preparation. This could be extended to fries as well.

- Re-arrange: Having customers pay before/after they eat.

- Re-arrange: Accommodating more customers by re-arranging the layout of the restaurant.

- Put to Another Use: Making the restaurant child-friendly by putting the available space to another use such as reserving some space especially for children.

- Similarly, can the restaurant offer something special to attract senior citizens, thus differentiating itself?

- Modifying: Modifying the cuisine to suit local tastes. The multinational restaurant chains such as McDonald's or KFC often does this in India.

- Substitute: Can the restaurant use people with special needs to serve or prepare food or handle some tasks such as at the cash counter, etc. There is a coffee chain, for example, that uses people with hearing impairments. Not only does this demonstrate sensitivity to the differently abled, but it is also practically prudent as it can decrease both costs and attrition rates.

CHALLENGING ASSUMPTIONS

The 'SCAMPER' technique is particularly effective when one combines it with established beliefs and assumptions. I always suggest to my teammates and colleagues to step back from the immediate issue or problem at hand, and ask some important questions about the assumptions that the team members individually or collectively have about the product, service, or situation.

It is always particularly effective to challenge assumptions when you are stuck in current thinking paradigms or have run out of ideas as the section on paradigm shift elucidated. We need to ask ourselves whether the aspects that have been assumed as crucial are really so, or are they just so because we've all become accustomed to them.

For example, do we really need people to drive a car, or waiters to serve at restaurants? Do we really need human agents to answer customer queries or can we look at alternatives? Do we really need the extant inventory management techniques or can we implement radically different ones?

SMALL ACTIONS, BIG IMPACT

Ideation techniques, when combined with an open mind, can help an individual or a company to break out of situations where their career or revenues are respectively stagnating. Indeed, the focus of many an executive coaching programme is to make them personally more effective by using such techniques both for themselves and their companies.

One can always change results by changing the way one approaches the tasks that lead to those results. One does not always have to make major changes or launch completely different products or enter new geographies. Very often, it can be simple changes in the product or service configuration that can lead to results that are significantly different. It is here that techniques such as 'SCAMPER' can help make a difference.

An environmentalist, I once met, pointed out that such techniques that look at multiple possibilities can help make a difference even in the context of larger global issues. For example, simple modifications in building materials, positions of a house's windows to let in more natural light, etc., can impact the carbon footprint of a residence, and if mandated or implemented across the board, can make a significant difference to the extent of global warming and such matters. So clearly, there is much power in such methods, if used effectively.

Chapter 7

From Strategy to Implementation

Strategy without tactics is the slowest route to victory,
tactics without strategy is the noise before defeat.
—Sun Tzu, ancient Chinese military strategist

When one considers strategy, Michael Porter was explicit: 'operational efficiency is not strategy'. What does this mean? It means that doing things better than others, for example, making better products, or even making comparable products at a lower cost, is not strategy. Why? It is only a temporary advantage. But strategy is what leads to a 'sustainable' competitive advantage.

In most markets, innovations can indeed be copied quickly; therefore, the management gurus state that improvement in operational efficiencies while being necessary, are not sufficient to achieve superior profit margins in the long-term. Operational efficiencies means your dieting has been successful, as Kenichi Ohmae may say, but it does not mean that you have a sustainable strength in the market.

Strategy entails the element of differentiation; or put in other words, you have to virtually create a market in which you are the only player, for you have to find a way in which your business or offering differs from the competition. This means that you have to make choices—for you can only be different by deciding what to do and what not to. You have to make choices in the nature and variety of products your business provides, the customer segments it serves, the channels through which it goes to market.

Porter was clear that strategy involves making trade-offs; while operational effectiveness did not. These tradeoffs, said Michael Porter, occur when 'more of one thing necessitates less of another'. Taking the example of airlines, he said that it could choose to serve meals during the flight but this would add to its costs and slow the turnaround time at the gate as the meals would need to be loaded; or it can choose not to serve meals, but obviously it could not do both without bearing major inefficiencies.

Let me put this slightly differently. Strategy can be said to mean the following: 'For (Who), we (do What) by (How).' The 'Who' here refers to the specific type of customers or client that your firm wishes to serve through its product or service. Hence, it refers to the industry category, the market segments, the types of clientele or demographic audience, etc. The 'What' is your product or service, and more importantly, the unique solution or benefits your company provide to the clients you have chosen to serve. The 'How' refers to the manner in which you deliver value. Is it online or at the store? What is the procedure, approach or method your company uses?

Now we move on to implementation. Once we have determined the tradeoffs (hence, the strategy), we now need to see whether the activities we do reinforce one another or not. Porter refers to the example of low-cost carrier Southwest Airlines and states.[1]

> Southwest's rapid gate turnaround, which allows frequent departures and greater use of aircraft, is essential to its high-convenience, low-cost positioning. But how does Southwest achieve it? Part of the answer lies in the company's well-paid gate and ground crews, whose productivity in turnarounds is enhanced by flexible union rules. But the bigger part of the answer lies in how Southwest performs other activities. With no meals, no seat assignment, and no interline baggage transfers, Southwest avoids having to perform activities that slow down other airlines. It selects airports and routes to avoid congestion that introduces delays. Southwest's strict limits on the type and length of routes make standardized aircraft possible: every aircraft Southwest turns is a Boeing 737.

---

[1] Adapted from Porter, Michael E., *Harvard Business Review*, Nov/Dec 1996.

So what does good implementation entail? It means that if an airline is choosing to be low-cost, every single element in the value chain must support this low-cost strategy. If there is even one element that does not align with a low-cost strategy, it means that there is a window of opportunity for someone else to come in and be still more efficient; hence out-competing the original player.

So when one speaks about implementation, once the strategy is framed, I generally advise teams to list down all the major activities that need to be undertaken. Each and every element now must be aligned to the strategy that has been decided; this is the crux of good implementation.

Let us stick with the airline example. We can consider the Indian low-cost carrier, Indigo, instead of Southwest for the sake of familiarity. What are the activities that are part of running an airline? Here are some major ones:

- Ticket booking
- The check-in procedure
- Baggage handling, storage and retrieval
- Fuelling aircraft
- Transporting passengers to the aircraft and back
- Flight and aircraft scheduling
- Aircraft parking
- Actually flying the plane
- Management of customers on board including serving them food and beverages
- Turn-around time at the gate
- Skills and capabilities of the crew and staff

- Handling call centre queries of all kinds including for lost baggage, etc.

- Maintenance of aircraft including management of spares

- Managing procurement

- Managing loyalty programmes

- Managing recruitment and selection

- Marketing and promotions

Everything matters. The airline needs to make sure that if it is to be successful with its low-cost strategy, then it is super-efficient in all elements and there is nothing that creates a dissonance; in this case, nothing that goes against a low cost strategy.

So, for example, if the airline needs to ensure a quick turn-around, it may need to ensure that all its staff are adequately trained and skilled to perform their activities highly efficiently, getting it right at the first instance and requiring no re-work. This may actually mean spending more initially on training, rather than less- because that is what the low-cost strategy needs.

Consider on the other hand, a company that expects highly efficient operations towards driving down costs, but does not spend adequately on training. The staff simply is not trained sufficiently well enough to support the quick turnaround; hence, the strategy begins to unravel. The training here could mean simple things such as opening the aircraft doors quickly, stashing away the trolleys that have been used to serve food and beverages, filling in the myriad paperwork that airline operators are required to do etc.

What are the other elements towards this low-cost strategy? The airline, for example, may not be able to pay commission to agents, for that adds to cost. It may not be able to cater to unique dietary needs of customers, but serve only standardized meals. It may need to get its customers to avoid carrying too much check-in luggage, so it may charge heftily for check-in luggage.

It may need to avoid loyalty or 'frequent flyer' programmes if administering these leads to increased costs. It may need to minimize on-board services if they similarly result in increased time and costs.

The bottom line is the implementation which involves listing down all the steps (especially the ones that add value) and making sure that all these align to the strategy. It may also include trying to eliminate activities that add to time and effort, but not to value. For example, avoiding paper-based boarding passes and moving to a completely digital check-in process (using mobile boarding passes) could save time.

LINK BETWEEN STRATEGY AND IMPLEMENTATION

So how does strategy and implementation link together? Put relatively simply, it is as follows:

First, you must make a choice, so that you have a clear and distinctive value proposition. Identify which customer segments and customer needs will you serve and at what relative price. Are you doing something different from others, i.e., providing a sustainable competitive advantage?

This is where your strategy also may mean saying no to some customers, so that you can better serve others. As an example, an automobile company like Audi may decide not to cater to the mass market so that it better serves the need of customers who buy a car for the 'status' it confers.

Micheal Porter says that it is actually these trade-offs which are an important source of profitability differences among rivals, for trade-offs make it difficult for rivals to copy what you do without compromising their own strategies. So, taking the case of Audi, it is the choice that it has made that prevents a Maruti Suzuki from competing against it, for it would be difficult for a Maruti to confer the same kind of status to the owner of an Audi. This is because Audi had chosen to stay away from a large segment of the population.

The iconic advertiser David Ogilvy says, 'The essence of strategy is sacrifice.' Writing in the *HBR*, David Collis and Michael Rukstad say, 'The trade-offs companies make are what distinguish them strategically from other firms[2].' In effect, your trade-offs *are* your strategy.

ENSURING ROBUST AND EFFECTIVE IMPLEMENTATION

This means managing your activities to deliver your key value proposition. There must be no dissonance in any activity. Furthering your competitive advantage lies in performing these activities differently and better than your competitors. It may mean selling online, for example, rather than through traditional brick and mortar stores. It may mean not using travel agents at all. These are the aspects that ultimately decide whether the company will succeed in its strategy; whether it can charge premium prices or to operate at lower cost.

---

[2] David J. Collis and Michael G. Rukstad, 'Can You Say What Your Strategy Is', *Harvard Business Review*, April 2008; https://hbr.org/2008/04/can-you-say-what-your-strategy-is, accessed on 24 October 2019.

VALIDATION

When one evaluates one's strategy, I suggest you consider asking yourself three fairly straightforward questions:

- **Does it help us say no to the certain prospects?** Does your strategy provide you with a method to select your audience or customer—one that wants that which you do best? Remember that a robust and narrow focus may make you the 'right choice' for your target customer. That is why an Audi, a Rolls Royce or a Harley Davidson hold so much charm for their fans.

- **Does it create strong barriers to entry?** Next, you have to ensure that your strategy leads to a sustainable advantage. Does the strategy of an Audi ensue that it does not make itself vulnerable to competition? Does it create boundaries that make it difficult for competitors to enter your space and do what your company does? Good strategy has to be hard to copy.

- **Does it result in fewer competitors?** This is very important. Can your strategic actions ensure that your firm actually reduces its direct competitors? This is where aspects of the 'blue ocean' come in—try and create new markets—where you are the only player.

Robust Implementation of Strategy Requires Robust KRAs and Effective Review Mechanisms

What are the key aspects to ensure that the strategy once decided translates into effective implementation on the ground?

I have seen that there are two crucial aspects:

- First, putting in place an effective review mechanism that includes holding effective meetings.

- Second, translating strategy into actionable key result areas (KRAs)/key performance indicators (KPIs) at both department and individual levels and then tracking their progress.

Let us look at the review mechanism first. The strategy translates into a business plan; and this must be periodically reviewed, often once a month.

The business plan review helps the company identify and address any bottlenecks in strategy implementation, assign or re-assign resources to achieve objectives, identify areas of improvement, track and implement quick fixes, if needed, etc. It also ensures that the new joiners who may not have been on-board during the original strategy formulation sessions are quickly on top of their work and know what is to be done.

What are the set of activities to ensure a good review? I have listed some of them here as follows:

Pre-meeting Preparation

- Agree and circulate the agenda among all the key personnel who must attend the meeting.

- Define the participant list and the roles and contributions expected from each participant.

- Circulate the pre-read at least three days before the meeting.

- Circulate any draft proposals well in advance.

Content (during the review meeting)

- Ensure all participants are on time.

- Always go through the previous agenda item and ensure previously agreed action items have been closed out.

- Stick to the agenda and items to be discussed.

- Try and understand all deviations comprehensively. Use a root-cause analysis approach and separate problems from their symptoms. Go behind each crucial number and data point and try to understand what is causing the data to depict or look like it does.

- Always benchmark both against the previous period as well as the target.

- Always look for trends, to pick up early warning signals. What are the patterns that you can discern? Separate these patterns from the noise.

- Address the root cause when you propose solutions. Always question, clarify, even challenge till you identify the root cause.

- Ensure that there is an identified 'action owner'; ensuring ownership is crucial.

- Do not focus only on the past; in fact, keep more time for deciding the future course of action.

Post the Meeting

- Follow up with action owners to ensure that the decided actions are implemented.
- Stick to the defined schedule for the next meeting.

Besides the business plan review, there are other review meetings to be held. These are the ones conducted by individual teams, functions and departments. Such reviews need to occur much more frequently, once a week is a good frequency. But different meetings must have different purposes.

Weekly Meetings

These could be held every Monday. They can comprise:

- An analysis of the previous week's activities: highlight all tactical successes and agree to where these can be duplicated, possibly in other territories or with other products. Similarly, understand all tactical failures to correct the actions next time.
- Define any emerging bottleneck and quickly take to management if needed. There is no point escalating when it is too late to do anything about it.

Monthly Review Meetings

This meeting must ideally be held towards the end of a month. In this meeting, do the following:

- Include a comprehensive review of the current month's performance, highlighting what went well and why, what didn't work and why. Review key KPIs/ KRAs and define corrective actions, if any.

- Define next month's activities in detail. Ensure the business plan objectives are being met through these actions.

The second important aspect is to work out the appropriate KRAs or KPIs. A related aspect is to define which data points will be looked at while deciding actions. Very often, when I have asked questions, the answers I have received have been ambiguous, and speculative in nature.

For example, when noticing that sales were stagnating or dropping, I was often told that the sales personnel were appearing demotivated; and this was the cause of the decline in Sales. I gradually learnt to ask how this conclusion had been arrived at; after all, a decline in motivation is at best a symptom, the real cause being 'why the motivation level had declined' and indeed, whether this was actually so.

What were the data points one could look at to check if this were indeed the case? Motivation is a behavioural or 'softer' trait which is difficult to quantify. Was this an excuse or was it a genuine reason? How could one judge motivation levels? Some of the parameters I learnt to look at to understand whether individuals or teams were indeed losing motivation are as follows:

- The number of calls the sales people were making per day or per week: Did these show any significant change?
- The conversion ratio—the number of leads converted into prospects: Was this showing any change?
- The attrition rate in a particular geography.
- The incentives earned: Were these showing any significant change?

There are, of course, other data points or indicators one could look at. The point is that one must verify what is going on by looking at certain data points or sets of data. The actions that one decides must be based on correct identification of the cause; if not, and one is relying on guesswork or hearsay and 'getting it right' depends on hit and trial, then this may end up in the company losing crucial time.

Similarly, taking another example, the strategy that a company decides could focus on innovation. But how can this translate into KPIs or KRAs? How can one track the level of innovation? Some indicators are:

- Number of patents filed.
- Number of new products being produced.
- Percentage of revenues coming from new products which have been introduced say in the last two years.
- Number of people dedicated to innovation in the firm and so on.

Chapter 8

Avoiding Assumptions and Biases

If I had asked people what they wanted,
they would have said faster horses.

—Henry Ford

In my experience of over a decade and a half, I have come to see that the biggest impediment to correct decision-making is not the absence of information or the lack of capability of an individual making a decision, but the fact that almost all individuals tend to make a variety of assumptions and have a variety of biases, about which they are mostly unconscious while taking decisions. Let me start by outlining some of the biases that I have often seen to occur in corporate settings. There has been plenty of research done around these, but it is worthwhile listing down the most common types of biases/assumptions to understand how familiar they actually are to all of us.

- **Avoidance of ambiguity effect:** The tendency to avoid options for which the probability of a favourable outcome is unknown. This is one of the chief reasons why innovations or new business models face challenges in adoption in many firms.

- **Status quo bias:** Related to the former one, this is a bias towards favouring the current situation or status quo and maintaining it due to loss aversion (fear of losing the current position and avoiding doing new things to avert risks of falling further back) and do nothing as a result. We tend to prefer what is familiar or 'the way we do things around here'. Both these biases have severe consequences on innovation and the ability of people or an organization to creatively solve needs and problems.

- **Anchoring bias:** One of the most common biases and something that almost all of us have seen play out at some time or the other, this bias manifests itself in people being influenced by information that is already known or that is first shown. It causes a kind of 'tunnel vision' (becoming blind to other information that may be conflicting) and considerably influencing the final decision-making. It also can be seen to be at work when sometimes we deliberately manipulate team members' minds by 'pre-loading' them with certain kinds of information or data.

- **Availability heuristic:** The tendency to overestimate the likelihood of events which have recently occurred and thus have greater 'availability' in memory. Besides recent occurrence, events which have been emotionally charged tend to be overestimated.

- **Bandwagon effect:** The tendency to do (or believe) things because many other people do (or believe) the same. Related to groupthink and herd behaviour, this manifests itself in shoppers purchasing a particular product because others do so, or avoid one for the same reason; financial brokers prefer the same stock, etc. Again, discourages a strategy where an individual or company tries to be different.

- **Base rate fallacy or base rate neglect:** The tendency to ignore base rate information (generic information or data) and focus on information that may be true only in a certain case. For example, marketers may assume a strong demand for a particular product based on last month's sales, but that demand may have arisen only due to some specific condition. One example of this was that post demonetization in India, there was a brief period in which sales through cards and e-wallets increased substantially, but this was followed by a return to the 'base rate' once the cash shortages in the Indian economy gradually reduced.

- **Self-serving bias**: This involves favouring decisions that enhance self-esteem. This results in attributing positive events to oneself and one's abilities. For example, a leader may feel that it was his leadership that brought about a particular outcome, while in reality, it may have been due to pure luck or the play of some other external factors.

- **Framing bias**: Another very common bias, it describes how individuals are often influenced by the way in which information is presented rather than the information itself. Good salesmen use this effectively, making statements such as 'our fund has delivered positive returns in three of the last five years', while avoiding any reference to the negative result that the fund obviously delivered for the other two years.

- **Planning fallacy**: The tendency to underestimate the task-completion time and to be over-optimistic.

- **Survivorship bias:** A very important bias that would-be startups should avoid. It refers to the tendency to pay attention to people or things that 'survived' and became successful, while forgetting all those who failed to succeed in a similar task. Successes and the people who achieved them are obviously more celebrated, but one must remember that many may have failed on the same path or with the same product.

- **Confirmation bias**: One of the most common and most researched biases, this is unfortunately one that seems to mostly affect senior management, especially when they are taking decisions. Research shows that we often believe what we want to believe by favouring information that confirms pre-existing beliefs or preconceptions. This bias results in the management looking for solutions that often conform to their existing beliefs or paradigms. This may mean putting more resources on an existing product, rather than venture to make new ones.

RECOGNIZING THE EXISTENCE OF BIASES AND ASSUMPTIONS

While it is easy to recognize some biases, a large number of biases are hidden. The first step to avoid biases and assumptions is to recognize that they are at work in our thinking or decision-making.

When you hear any of the following statements, I suggest you stop for a moment and take a step back for these statements reflect that biases or assumptions are at work and perhaps cloud the decision-making process:

'We know what the customers want.'

'That's the way we've always done it.'

'This group of customers is just too demanding.'

'Senior management won't let approve this.'

'It's too ambiguous, we need to quantify it and present it in a spreadsheet.'

'How do we know it would even work?'

'Our development cycles are too long for that.'

'Let me check with my superior/manager.'

'That idea won't work.'

'It's already been done.'

'Nobody would allow it.'

'This is not a creative organization.'

'We can look at that next quarter/next year.'

'Not everybody believes in innovation.'

'There's no budget for this.'

'Let's do a survey first.'

'There are too many issues for that to work.'

How many times have you heard such statements being made? I remember that especially in the early part of my career. When I used to go to my director with an idea, I was often told, 'It's a great idea, but let's do that next year'.

AVOIDING ASSUMPTIONS AND BIASES

Making the right decisions is crucial for all managers today; the ability to process all the prior knowledge one has, the new information that one can gather and then decide what to do is a very important skill. So, how does one avoid making assumptions, especially ones that may lead to the wrong answers?

First, one should approach problems in a structured manner. 'Structured problem-solving' is imperative for today's corporate manager or consultant. Typical structured approaches involve one or both of the following (indeed, is part of the training that new recruits are put through by most of the management consultancy firms):

- Preparing MECE charts (MECE standing for Mutually Exclusive but Collectively Exhaustive)
- Conducting an Ishikawa or Fishbone Analysis of the given matter. Ishikawa diagrams were popularized in

the 1960s by Kaoru Ishikawa, another Japanese 'management guru', who pioneered quality management processes in the Kawasaki shipyards. While the basic concept was first reportedly used even earlier, Ishikawa used them systematically to ensure it emerged as one of the basic tools of quality control.

It is also known as a 'fishbone diagram' because of its shape, similar to the side view of a fish skeleton with the problem statement being at the 'head' and the bones of the fish representing all the streams of thoughts and their branches.

MECE is a method of grouping information into elements that are mutually exclusive and collectively exhaustive, as the acronym suggests. Hence, the idea is to put the information or thoughts one has into 'buckets' that are distinct from one another, but comprehensive in scope. There should be no overlapping between buckets and put together, all the buckets should cover all possible aspects of the issue.

For example, let us consider issues of cost. One can look at all possible ways to reduce cost, and the different ways would constitute separate buckets.

Strategy consultants have for long used this framework segregate a client's problems into logical data categories that can be analysed systematically and closely by those working on the project. Besides its use by consultants, many well-known frameworks, including Cost-Benefit Analysis, the 4Cs or the 7S approach, Porter's Five Forces, etc., have the MECE principle at their core.

ISSUE TREES

How is the MECE framework used to solve problems or issues? The framework involves creating an 'issue tree' by arranging all the information that you may have and then divide this information into all possible issues and sub-issues (which represent the branches of the tree). An issue tree is particularly helpful for solving large and complex problems as it facilitates splitting them up into smaller, solvable problems. After all, the best problem solvers know how to 'Simplify and simplify'.

Let us now look at a common area where one can use such a framework. One of the most common reasons where we may adopt a structured approach is to improve profitability.

Let us first write down a problem statement, considering the example of a restaurant business that wishes to be more profitable. So let us first start by therefore writing: 'How can we make the restaurant profitable?' The first branches of the tree would be simple, generic and broad enough categories: 'Increase revenue' and 'Reduce costs'. The second level would focus on the 'How' of these two generic areas; hence, 'How to increase revenue?' and 'How to reduce costs?' on the other.

Now brainstorm within the team on various possibilities to increase revenues. Arrange the ideas in categories or buckets. The answers under 'Increase revenue' would be 'Increase the number of orders' and 'Increase the prices of items'. The answers under 'Reduce costs' could include as examples aspects such as 'Reduce salary expenditures', 'Reduce rental', and 'Reduce raw material expenses'. You are free to add to this list. On the third level, the issue tree would tackle the aspects we have identified earlier in greater detail.

Let us start with 'How to increase the number of orders?' One way to increase orders could be to change the location itself of the restaurant; after all someone wise was very accurate in saying the three success factors in such a business are 'Location, location, location'! Another way to increase sales can be to create greater awareness through a strong marketing campaign so that the restaurant becomes more widely known. Now let us look at the costs side. We have the main head 'reduce salary expenditures'. How can this be done? There are many possibilities such as:

- Identify and reduce redundancies
- Shift the location to an area where it is possible to hire staff for a lower amount
- Hire the types of personnel that cost less, etc.

Let us now take the objective of 'reducing raw material expenses'. How can we do this?

We can try the following:

- Re-negotiate with our existing vendors
- Change the vendor
- Change the ingredients we use, etc.

How does an issue tree help? It enables consultants to consider all options separately and exclusively and suggest the best option to the client. It helps to create a common understanding among team members about the problem-solving framework and focus on team efforts. As much has been written about these two techniques, I would like to point out some other pre-requisites that I feel have often been neglected.

PROBLEMS AND SYMPTOMS

When faced with any issue that requires a solution, the first crucial aspect is to separate problems from the symptoms. This is often neglected; and it is here that most problem-solvers or strategists go wrong.

Let's suppose someone comes to a doctor complaining of fever. The doctor does not start speculating what is wrong with his patient. She recognizes the fever as it denotes only a symptom. She identifies the cause of the fever thereafter.

A good doctor now goes about her work in a structured manner. She records her observations, some of which are obtained by asking the patient a number of questions. These observations would typically include aspects such the person's temperature, blood pressure, number of days during which the fever persisted, any other accompanying symptoms, etc. If required, she might ask the patient to undergo a medical test to investigate the cause of the fever. It is only after these tests and observations that the doctor feels confident enough to diagnose the cause of the fever. This is the 'scientific approach' of diagnosis.

Unfortunately, many management practitioners deviate from such an approach. They fail at the initial stage itself, i.e., understanding the symptoms. Even if they do recognize these to be symptoms, they start speculating about what the causes are and start basing their actions on such speculations.

Let us consider two common management-related issues. One can be a company that faces declining or stagnant sales; or a situation where sales are growing, but not as faster as before and not as fast as the management would like them to grow. Another situation is a company facing attrition of its employees. What are these two situations examples of? They are both NOT problems, they are symptoms of problems which need to be recognized.

If these are merely symptoms, what then is the real issue or problem? In the examples above, the problem is:

- The reason WHY sales are stagnating, declining or not growing fast enough
- The reason WHY the company is facing attrition

Let us examine the issue of sales closely. What could be the reason for the falling or stagnating sales? It could be one or more of the following:

- The sales force is not performing well enough, which in turn could be due to capability issues or due to their incentives not being aligned well enough
- The product has itself become obsolete, hence faces declining demand
- The distribution model is not optimal
- A major competitor has undertaken an action that has affected the company's sales
- The preferences of the consumer has gradually changed away from the particular product

Many companies assume that changing the price of the product, typically lowering it, will address the issue. But it may well fail, especially if the product has itself become obsolete or the consumer tastes have changed (as they often do in today's world).

Consider the case of Nokia, which once had a global market share of well over 50 per cent in feature phones. It failed to see that the market was undergoing a change and that the consumer wanted a 'smartphone'; hence, the company slowly but surely lost its market. Merely adjusting the price was not a solution that would work.

A 'SYSTEMS THINKING' APPROACH

Now, given the range of these possible solutions outlined earlier, the company must perform rigorous analysis to understand the real root cause. Is it a pricing issue or a distribution one or the more fundamental change in consumer preferences?

Peter Michael Senge (born 1947) is an American systems scientist who is a senior lecturer at the MIT Sloan School of Management, co-faculty at the New England Complex Systems Institute, and the founder of the Society for Organizational Learning. He is best known as the author of the book *The Fifth Discipline: The Art and Practice of the Learning Organization.*

In 1997, *HBR* identified this work as one of the seminal management books of the previous 75 years. Senge was named 'Strategist of the Century' by the *Journal of Business Strategy*, which said that he was one of the very few people who 'had the greatest impact on the way we conduct business today'.

When we speak about finding the root cause through analysis, Peter Senge, describes this as 'systems thinking'. The proximate reason is often not the real reason for the manifested phenomena, but there are deeper, systemic issues that need to be addressed. For example, declining sales is not the fault of the salesman. The company must seek and address the underlying real issue.

Senge goes on to say that 'systems thinking' has sometimes been called the 'second dismal science' (Economics being the original dismal one, after Robert Malthus understood that economic productivity was subject to diminishing returns and stated that you could 'not grow the world's food supply in a flowerpot'). Why so? The easiest and most proximate cause may not be the real one; a lot of time and effort needs to be invested to find the actual cause. Just like the doctor who notes observations and then prescribes tests, the organization facing a situation of declining/stagnating sales must carefully note observations and conduct research ('tests') followed by rigorous analysis. This may include:

- Understanding whether there is a secular decline in sales period-on-period or across geographies or is it that the decline is a temporary blip and limited to particular geographies

- Have competitors resorted to any specific actions? This could include a change in their pricing or the introduction of a new product in the market

- What are the prevalent economic conditions? For example, tractor sales are influenced by sowing activity, which in turn, is influenced by monsoon patterns

- Has there been a change in any parameter/strategy that the company had earlier adopted, for example, changes in loyalty programmes, incentives to salespeople or distributors, etc.

Once the root cause is found, taking remedial actions is actually easy. The crux, therefore, is not falling prey to assumptions and reactive approaches, but relying on careful observation and analysis. Don't assume things and don't jump to conclusions!

There are two other techniques that help avoid biases and assumptions. One is the 'root cause' analysis popularized by Taiichi Ohno, the father of the Toyota Production System; he was also known for his 'Ten Percepts'.

Taiichi Ohno's 'Ten Precepts' to Think and Act to Win

1. You are a cost. First reduce waste.

2. First say, 'I can do it.' And try before everything.

3. The workplace is a teacher. You can find answers only in the workplace.

4. Do anything immediately. Starting something right now is the only way to win.

5. Once you start something, persevere with it. Do not give up until you finish it.

6. Explain difficult things in an easy-to-understand manner. Repeat things that are easy to understand.

7. Waste is hidden. Do not hide it. Make problems visible.

8. Valueless motions are equal to shortening one's life.

9. Re-improve what was improved for further improvement.

10. Wisdom is given equally to everybody. The point is whether one can exercise it.

Ohno was clear in stating that finding the actual root cause of anything is the key to a lasting solution. What do we often do when we spot a leak? We may put a bucket below the dripping water. This is however clearly a temporary solution. The root cause of the leak may well be some damage in the roof; hence, repairing the roof is a lasting solution in this case. Taiichi Ohno was fond of the following example in the context of root causes.

- 'Why did the robot stop?' The circuit has overloaded, causing a fuse to blow.

- 'Why is the circuit overloaded?' There was insufficient lubrication on the bearings, so they locked up.

- 'Why was there insufficient lubrication on the bearings?' The oil pump on the robot is not circulating sufficient oil.

- 'Why is the pump not circulating sufficient oil?' The pump intake is clogged with metal shavings.

- 'Why is the intake clogged with metal shavings?' There is no filter on the pump.

'The root cause of any problem is the key to a lasting solution,' Ohno said. Why have I chosen this example?

First, the initial occurrence of a circuit being overloaded is something we have all experienced, hence, the example is familiar to most of us and causes the fuse to trip. Almost all our houses today have Miniature Circuit Breakers (MCBs) and at some time or the other, we have experienced a situation when it trips.

What do we normally do when it trips? Without batting an eyelid, we go and turn the circuit back on. But this is not necessarily the right thing. For we have not understood the reason why it tripped. Now since we have not really understood the 'why', there is a good chance that we may see the circuit tripping again, if the condition happens again. The circuit tripping is merely the symptom, we have to understand where the problem lies.

That involves probing more, and asking a few 'Whys'. This is Ohno's approach—he says ask 'why' five times, and you may eventually come to the root cause.

So the next time you experience the circuit in your house tripping, try to probe deeper!

Second, I have used this example, but it eventually shows that a very small, mundane thing (there not being a filter) caused a failure of the entire system (the robot as a whole). Real-life situations are often like that.

It does not take expensive, difficult, hard to obtain things to fix most issues. A very small action or piece of information or equipment may well be all that is required. In Taiichi Ohno's example, all that was needed was a small filter on the pump. Very often, such small things make all the difference.

CEO Speak: Ashok Ramachandran, President & CEO, Schindler India Pvt Ltd

Ashok Ramachandran recently was recognized by the *Economic Times*' '40 under 40' initiative; he is the President and CEO of Schindler India Pvt Ltd, part of the multi-national Schindler group, which was founded in 1874 in Lucerne, Switzerland, and is today one of the world's leading providers of elevators, escalators, and moving walks, as well as maintenance and modernization services. The Group has over 1,000 branch offices in more than 100 countries, as well as production sites and research and development facilities in the US, Brazil, Europe, China, and India.

Ashok has worked in multiple locations worldwide, in leadership roles. I spoke to him on the matter of biases and assumptions and whether there were occasions where the consumer surprised him or his company; or when the market threw up results contrary to expectations. This is what he had to say: 'In my experience of over a decade of working in various countries, this is very common. Changes and surprises are the name of the game. We launched in India our Digital and IoT (Internet of Things) based products in India in late 2018. Before and during the launch, most people within and outside the organization whom we spoke with about this were very sceptical.... We were told that in India this would not work and people still only choose what is lowest in price. When we launched, we were also very apprehensive and hence made sure that we don't recruit too many people to sell and brand these products.'

He continues, 'But the way the market welcomed us and started buying the IoT products and services, it really surprised us. Within just six months, we were able to connect more than 5,000 elevators using the IoT platform and the team had also ramped us rapidly to keep up with the demand. This was a really positive surprise; the overwhelming market reaction was entirely unexpected!'

I also wanted to understand from him as to how his company goes about the process of strategy and innovation, including avoiding such biases and assumptions. He replied, 'Well, I can only talk about the geographies in Schindler that I worked and not about the global Schindler approach. But overall, we are a decentralised company and each branch or country head is given freedom to do things. When I was managing a branch in Australia, I launched my first three-year strategy. This was very much a bottom -up approach. We formed a core team of 30 managers and influencers. I have also always ensured that we include two to three young high potential talented individuals who will not only learn by being in such forums but also contribute new and different ideas. During the bottom-up approach, customer, employee and stakeholder feedbacks are sought. All this becomes an input when we finally work on the strategy days ensuring that the voice of the customer is paramount, not our perceptions or biases. The 'Strategy days' could be usually a two-three day conference in which we form smaller groups to formulate what we want to achieve in a three year time horizon; and how we plan to get to where we want'.

He makes the point that, 'The trick about doing such things is to not rely on templates only or a template-based approach to have say 20 actions, but to concentrate on and push five to six key initiatives. Saying "No" to many of the ideas is the toughest part. But once you finalize the plan, then it is about relentless execution. This is where most companies fail. I usually have a task force for each initiative with one person responsible along with the team. This ensures buy-in and speed of execution. Before we even started sessions on strategy, I also take some basic classes on strategic thinking. All this helps to ensure we have a solid achievable strategy in place. For example, in India, we have established a five year strategy—"Bigger, Faster, Fitter" is the war cry and we are now making a clear road map on how to get there.'

He also adds some interesting points: 'I have mentioned above both the details of strategy that worked and common pitfalls. But let me tell you the most important part of strategy is leadership. You need a strong yet humble leader. Second, strategic focus is not very common. Most people are used to thinking short term and fire-fighting. So one has to spend time making people understand why strategy is important and what value addition it brings for them. Here is one example of something which may be useful to know and learn. This was when I joined Schindler Vietnam as Managing Director.

'When I arrived in Schindler Vietnam, it was in a turnaround mode and I had just turned 31 years old. We were far from meeting our targets and the issues were further compounded by massive code of conduct-related issues, safety issues on job sites and people leaving the organization. The morale was far from good and few were working with any kind of enthusiasm. I knew I was going to have a tough time, but still wasn't really expecting the extent of issues I did face. Nevertheless, I was ready for this and no looking back. We always read about how we need to put people first and this was the right environment for doing that.

'My key initiative, therefore, was relating to people. I realized the need to first have a strong local management team; which I set out to do immediately. I had to make sure I find local Vietnamese talent as filling the organization with expatriate hires would not give much confidence to the talented local employees. I first got a strong head of Human Resources who was American trained Vietnamese and subsequently, a very talented Chief Financial Officer (CFO); then moving on to handpick people for key operational roles.

'To stop the attrition, I personally had a one-on-one with each of the high performers, trying to instil a sense of vision and purpose within them, while at the same time motivating them that we would become a top performing company. I stoked their nationalistic feelings that they as Vietnamese could not lose; and gradually the efforts paid off. Within a couple of years, we became the talk of the town within and outside Vietnam; and internally within Schindler, we won the Best Country Award for 2014 with many of our initiatives being replicated as "Best Demonstrated Practice" across the company. There are many such examples of people that I personally coached and developed who were all local Vietnamese talent. Whenever people ask me about my best achievements in my career, I always feel it's the people that I developed in the company.

'Related to this was another initiative- we established an Apprenticeship and Training centre in 2014. We learnt from best practices for this from across the world and developed our own curriculum along with a top local college.

The curriculum included training in English, culture, safety and customer excellence. All this was completely new in Vietnam and employees and customers were amazed at how we did things differently. Soon even our competitors copied us! The programme became popular with other industries too and we had visits from them to learn about what we do and how we did it. I personally met the apprentices every quarter and ensured that they were inspired and motivated to go above and beyond. Many of the apprentices now have become managers and leaders not just in Vietnam but in other Schindler operations worldwide.'

LAUNCH SOFTLY, BUT LISTEN VERY CAREFULLY

Theodore Roosevelt, a well-known former American President is credited to have advised, 'Speak softly, but carry a big stick'. Taking a leaf from this, I would always advise corporate executives embarking on a new product launch or would-be entrepreneurs starting a new venture to 'Launch softly, but listen very carefully'.

A successful way to avoid assumptions and biases is to use 'soft launches' or 'beta versions'. This is again something that Google states it does, going on to refer to a 'soft opening' even if starting a new restaurant. It says that instead of hoping everything is perfect and calling for a grand opening, a new restaurant can consider a few days where they invite selected people in, learn what works and discover the customers liking.

Google claims that early in their history, they released some of our products as 'beta launches' and then made rapid iterations as users provided feedback. It provides the example of its Android mobile operating system as a good example of this approach. The operating system was launched in 2008, and then improved continuously through feedback from the more than 1 billion active Android users in the world.

What is important here is to listen to the feedback and the voice of the customer. This is a powerful tool to avoid assumptions around what the owner of the business feels the customer would like or the consumer prefers, etc. It also gives him a better understanding of possible challenges that could crop up, including quality variations, etc.

I once had occasion to advise a couple of entrepreneurs who wished to provide a battery-operated eco-friendly solution to customers wanting last mile connectivity from New Delhi's metro stations to their places of residence, study or work.

I suggested that they start a trial service where users could avail the service at a minimal cost initially and provide feedback. There were many interesting learnings including users not knowing how to switch off the meter that recorded consumption and thus claiming to have been over-charged to wide variations in usage patterns at different times of the day, etc. All these were very different from what I and the founders thought would happen—the trial had busted our assumptions!

Let's end with a story that Simon Sanek, the now famous author of 'Start with Why' mentions in his book about a group of American automobile executives who had gone to Japan to see a Japanese assembly line. At the end of the assembly line, the automobile's doors were put on the hinges, the same as in United States. But the executives noticed that something was missing.

In the United States, a worker on the assembly line would take a rubber mallet and tap the edges of the door to ensure that it fit perfectly. In Japan, there was no such person!

Did the Japanese have deficient quality control processes? Were they compromising on quality and safety?

The American auto executives decided to ask. They queried therefore as to how the Japanese were sure the door fit perfectly if it wasn't being tested manually.

Their Japanese guide looked at them and smiled. 'We make sure it fits when we design it.'

In the Japanese way of doing things, they ensured that the engineering was good enough from the beginning. If they didn't achieve their desired outcome, they understood it was because of a decision they made at the start of the process—the design itself.

Simon Sinek goes on to postulate: 'The Japanese doors are likely to last longer and maybe even be more structurally sound in an accident. All this for no other reason than they ensured the pieces fit from the start.

'What the American automakers did with their rubber mallets is a metaphor for how so many people and organizations lead. When faced with a result that doesn't go according to plan, a series of perfectly effective short-term tactics are used until the desired outcome is achieved. But how structurally sound are those solutions?'

This is exactly what we must ponder over.

Chapter 9

Influencing Others: The Birbal Way

Tell the truth, but make it fascinating.

—David Ogilvy

In my experience, there are few more effective ways to motivate others in your team or outside; or be able to convince or influence others than the medium of 'storytelling'. In fact, storytelling has been called a 'judicious use of emotion for a strategic purpose'; the purpose in this case is to motivate, gain commitment or change others' beliefs.

Perhaps the best examples of this playing out are the witty court jesters that have become part of Indian folkfore. Many of us will surely recall the stories of Akbar and Birbal, Krishnadeva Raya and Tenali Rama, etc.

Note how the fame of these witty ministers is based on how they effectively told a story to convince the emperor; very often this involved convincing the powerful emperor that he was wrong. Do you think that Birbal would have achieved the same objective had he thrown facts and data at the emperor?

It is more likely that the emperor, instead of being convinced, would have thrown Birbal into prison! The fact that Birbal, Tenali Rama and others used a different medium—one of effective storytelling—that made them and their stories so popular down the ages.

THE POWERFUL STORY

As in for other strategic matters, success is the outcome of careful thought and planning. So also in the case of telling stories in a corporate setting. One should carefully think of the message that one wishes to convey and how the story can be made effective.

Story-telling works best if the audience, the story's objective and the channels you use to tell it are carefully considered in advance. The audience often determines the choice of channels and the way you narrate the story, which would depend on whether the audience comprises your colleagues or your customers or investors.

There are some characteristics of powerful stories:

- The story structure comprises a particular individual, his/ her goal, and the challenge. The way in which the individual approaches the challenge is full of drama, with turning points, ups and downs, and finally, the denouement.

  Why is this important? Remember, that whatever your company or institute is doing, be it earning profits or helping others, it is ultimately people that drive results and get things done. Hence, powerful stories tap into the motivations of people.

- The stories are designed to trigger emotional responses. Hence, the story must have sufficient 'conflict' built in; the stakes should be high so that the audience feels the pain of defeat and the triumph of victory.

  The story should be unique and authentic; appealing to the audience's sense of purpose, loyalty, their pride etc. While they should indeed be unique, authenticity is also important, in the sense of avoiding manipulation or alteration of what really happened, any fabrication of data, or role exaggerations, etc.

- Powerful tools and techniques can be incorporated including use of analogies and metaphors.

- Powerful stories go beyond just telling to ensure that people can relate with them. The narratives and incidents help transcend generic keywords and make people feel that they are in the shoes of the protagonist.

- They help put a face to an issue and help people connect to deeper issues by humanizing them. For example, whenever you wish to draw attention of an audience to the plight of a certain community or group of people, telling the story of one individual in that group, people connect much more than if you speak about the community as a whole; and the individual you choose must therefore be real and relatable.

Putting a face to an issue is very helpful when one wants to highlight some specific aspect. For example, just presenting data, figures or statistics does not always make an impression. People can contradict the statistics themselves, or the interpretation of data, or the manner in which it has been presented.

Let us consider the example of a person who wanted to highlight the importance of not using mobile phones while driving. He can choose to state the following:

- 'Data shows that so many thousands of accidents happen when people use mobile phones while driving.'
- 'Research shows that using mobile phones can shorten your reaction time by so many seconds.'

Or, he can tell a story. Let us say it goes thus:

Nitika had worked hard while preparing for her Common Admission Test (CAT) exam that serves to select students into India's prestigious Indian Institutes of Management (IIMs). She had joined a coaching institute and diligently attended all her classes, tests and completed all her assignments.

She was the only child of her aging parents and she knew how much they had sacrificed for her. Despite struggling with their finances, they had enrolled her into a coaching institute, barely managing to pay the fees in instalments; more expenses were required to fill up all the forms for the different institutes that accepted the CAT score. Nitika was keen to give it her best shot and hoped to make her parents proud.

The CAT exam had gone well and Nitika was hopeful. The day of the result dawned and Nitika chewed her fingers almost throughout the day. Towards the evening, she had to go to the market to pick up her provisions for the weekend. She got on her scooty and made her way to the market.

Suddenly, she received a call. It was her friend who was checking on the result through her laptop. Nitika knew that the call was to inform her about her result. Ears and mind fully glued to what her friend was saying while she drove, she failed to notice a small boy come onto the road. Suddenly, she saw him. She braked hard. Her scooty skidded; she could do nothing. The phone flew from her hand as her scooty hit something hard. Nitika had lost consciousness.

Which do you think is more effective in communicating the perils of using a mobile phone while driving?

Apart from trying to 'humanize' data, I have found that stories are particularly effective when you are trying to initiate some kind of organizational change. In this case, it helps immensely to use relatable characters like fellow employees, rather than stories of heroes or superstars.

I remember a time when I was trying to convince people to use the then relatively new technology of AI more in the organization. I narrated a story about a skit performed by the children of the employees.

This skit by itself had nothing to do with the technology, and there was one scene in which two young boys are complaining about their busy lives, saying they have no free time to do what they like. They say they spend too much time with their studies and their homework leaves them with little spare time. This prompts one of them to remark to the other that he has discovered a faster way of getting it done saying, 'Artificial Intelligence *to hain na*' (we have Artificial Intelligence with us).

This purely off-the-cuff remark from one of the two young boys illustrates a core benefit of AI as a technology. It can speed up the doing of mundane, everyday, boring, repetitive tasks leaving you time for more value-added or enjoyable stuff. The young boy wished to use it for his homework!

Hence, simplify and make everything relatable. For example, an NGO can try and show that the price of a cup of tea can help buy a book for a needy child.

I remember a particular presentation from an external consultant that I was sitting through. The presenter wanted my company to approve a project to provide drinking water to the people of the desert area of Barmer, Rajasthan, a noble project but costing as much as ₹100 crores. Wasn't it far too much?

The presenter was able to get the entire audience to his side by putting the statistic in a much more simple and relatable way—that the cost equated to providing everyone in the district quality drinking water for a period of seven years at just approximately ₹1,000 per year. That figure was far more relatable; people realized that they paid much more per year for drinking water at their homes. So the project, looked at in individual terms, was not so expensive after all.

FROM THE SPECIFIC TO THE UNIVERSAL

A good story, therefore, focuses on specific matters, a particular issue or an individual and his particular struggles. However, the good storyteller finds a way to make that specific aspect universal and applicable across time and space. Remember, that all individuals have similar aspirations, similar fears, similar desires and often similar strengths and weaknesses.

Guru Nanak was the founder of Sikhism and the first Guru of the Sikhs. He was once in Hardwar in today's Uttarakhand, which as we know is a sacred city. There were many people taking a dip in the holy Ganga; and Guru Nanak joined the crowd.

He suddenly noticed a priest turning to one side and throwing water towards the rising sun. The Guru was unable to reign in his curiosity and asked the priest what his actions were for. The priest puffed himself up and said, 'I am throwing the water towards my ancestors in heaven so that they may partake of the holy water'. The Guru immediately turned to the opposite direction and started repeating the priest's actions.

The priest shouted, 'What are you doing? You are facing the wrong way!' 'Nay,' said the Guru, 'I am facing my fields in the Punjab which are reeling from a drought. If the water you cast can reach your ancestors, I am sure the water I cast from here will reach my fields as well.'

The Guru's story is timeless and universal; illustrating the pit-falls of performing actions blindly, without any consideration of logic or rationality. It is equally applicable to a corporate setting where one sometimes is expected to blindly follow authority.

In this case, the Guru was trying to illustrate the pitfalls of acting without thinking. There can be many themes to a story—such as reliability, quality, innovation, collaboration, etc. Think of effective stories you may have to bring out the importance of these aspects! For, it is far more effective to motivate employees towards these goals through the medium of storytelling, rather than putting together a speech on their importance.

Audiences remember stories much more than they remember words. Many who heard my story about the two boys and their homework I mentioned above came up to me months or even a few years later, stating that they remembered the story I told them; which in turn helped them remember the concept.

Many companies on their websites or elsewhere share pas-sionate stories of their founders and how they started the firm. These stories build the emotional connect of the brand with the user. They 'humanize' the company, trying to show the customer that their founder faced almost insurmountable odds and rose to the occasion, doing something that made the world a better place; or at least did something that brought convenience to its customers.

The story of tractor maker John Deere and how he brought the steel ploughshare into use is one; the stories of McDonald's Ray Kroc or Colonel Sanders of KFC being others. Many successful authors too have stories of their rejections, before producing a bestseller.

STORIES TO BRING CHANGE

As I mentioned earlier, storytelling is particularly effective when trying to implement some kind of change in the organization. It is far too presumptuous to expect that employees will be convinced of change only by showing them copious amounts of data, numbers, statistics, analytics, etc., and worse, by reducing all these into a PowerPoint presentation. Those who wish to be change agents must engage through convincing dialogues, use of analogies and effective stories.

Indeed, Steve Jobs was one of the pioneers in the use of simple images and one line concepts to support his verbal storytelling. The concept of TED Talks is almost wholly built around the premise of storytelling. Top class speakers or innovators have been invited to come forth and speak in simple narratives, using stories and powerful imagery to convey their message.

Great leaders have often recognized that human centredness and human connections need to go first, well before numbers and statistics, and before concepts and strategies. Why? It is first important to connect with your customers or your audience and then get down to business.

A great example of how companies strive to bring about this 'connectedness' is the well-known 'Dear Holly' advertisement for Google Chrome. (You can see it on YouTube.) The advertisement is all about the company connecting with the user, to bring about strong bonds and an emotional attachment.

While the advertisement is like a series of disparate images of a little girl growing up, it has a very strong narrative built on an emotional connect; that of a father recounting his memories of his daughter's first years. The product is actually in the background, not in the forefront, but is the common thread to all the years that the father and daughter have shared together.

STORIES TO MARKET PRODUCTS

Storytelling is also a highly effective way to market products and is especially useful in the context of marketing handmade products including handicrafts made by rural artisans. Many companies are using this medium to speak about the composition of the artisanal product, how it was made, the life of the artisans, etc.

One initiative which has used the art of storytelling for this purpose is that of the global e-commerce giant Amazon. The company launched an ambitious programme to enable rural artisans to list their products on their platform a few years ago, called *Kala Haat* (literally 'Marketplace of Skills').

Amazon India decided to tour the country to directly communicate with local artisans, to help them overcome their doubts and fears, if any, of using the online e-commerce model for sales and to explain the world of opportunities that online sales could open up.

Artisans were given presentations detailing how to go onboard and sell products online, fetch an appropriate price for their unique hand-crafted products, market their products online, the extent of Amazon's network, the seller support they offer, how to maximise their reach to Amazon's vast audiences and logistics.

All products listed by artisans and weavers are available through the 'Handloom & Handicraft' store on Amazon.in. Launched in 2016, the store aims at bringing the handicrafts and handlooms of India, across categories, encompassing sarees, jewellery, handbags, shoes, etc., to a wide audience.

Along with the products were the stories—an elaborate description about how it was made and the story behind each product. The storytelling approach was taken forward further with Amazon allowing the sellers to outline their success stories, including their experiences with Amazon on its website. (You can take a look at some of them here: https://services.amazon.in/resources/seller-success-stories.html.)

FACTS TELL, BUT STORIES SELL

So indeed, if you are a marketer and wish to sell just about anything, you have to learn the art of storytelling!

There is much truth in the aphorism, 'Facts tell, stories sell'. Where all can you use these stories?

- If you have a website, use the 'About Us' page to tell a story. This is important to get people to buy into your brand or philosophy, the 'why' you are doing and what you are doing.

- You can further this communication through webinars, increasingly using it to connect with the desired audience at a deeper level and to incite trust.

- Using social media, blog posts or podcasts to stay engaged with your audience on a regular basis.

Telling a Good Story

Your story can follow the following structure to be effective in a corporate setting: you have a protagonist who has a particular ambition or goal that he wishes to achieve; he/ she faces certain obstacles along the way; and finally he/she succeeds in overcoming them to reach a transformative outcome. The greater the odds, the more effective is the story. Remember, everyone loves the underdog!

The Goal

Your story can start by providing a background of the protagonist and his/her goal—what the protagonist wishes to achieve. For example, it can be someone who starts off by selling lemonade at a street corner at a university campus and wishes to establish a business on these lines.

The Protagonist's Motivations, Desires and Feelings

Besides the overall goal, do share the protagonist's thoughts and feelings as well; what his/her motivations are. Why did he start this particular business? Was he moved by something?

For example, it could be that the protagonist had to earn extra income due to extenuating family circumstances; the difficulties he/she faced in making ends meet, etc.; or some other motivations like providing something that he felt would make a difference.

A start-up I was in touch with wished to make high quality gel mattresses as the founder was moved by the fact that his grandmother wanted a comfortable mattress but couldn't find one.

While some of the protagonist's motivations may be intensely private, it is always better to share this as it helps one to connect with the audience, who might relate more to a story that appears genuine.

How do you find what your internal motivations are? Start with your ambition and goal and keep asking yourself, 'What makes me want this,' until you understand what is pushing you.

The Obstacles

Now you can outline the obstacles you faced. This could be financial; it could be lack of support from your peers and family; it could be competition or anything else that stood in your way.

It is important for the audience to feel in your shoes at this moment, so provide them sufficient details. Who or what was opposing you?

For example, a friend who had started a snack counter found that the *hafta* he was asked by the local police made his business unviable. He had to find a way around this.

How You Achieve Your Goal

Now provide the audience details of how you went about achieving what you did.

Is there some new opportunity you grasped? Some new way you found? Something that kept you motivated?

An example could be using e-commerce platforms to reach a wider audience or getting some kind of help from a friend or spotting a new niche in the market

Resolution

Finally, the story must have a resolution. This is what was actually achieved. How far did you succeed? Did you reach your goal?

For example, a student who wished to make it to one of the top Indian Institutes of Management (IITs) or Indian Institutes of Management (IIMs) may have finally achieved his goal, perhaps after three or four attempts.

Or a mountain climber wishing to reach a particular summit might finally succeed after several attempts.

But this is important. The achievement is not the only thing you speak about. You must speak about the 'inner achievement' as well, how the success of achieving the goal made you a different person. How did it make you feel? How did it result in achieving your inner desires? For example, the founder of a start-up that has done well could speak about the inner confidence he/she had obtained; the respect he had earned from his peers; and how he rose in the eyes of his parents.

Hence the elements of a good story include the following aspects:

1. New Opportunity
2. The Plan
3. External Achievement
4. Internal Transformation

SO WHY DO STORIES WORK?

There is a strong physiological reason that makes stories work. Our body responds to them in ways that we are gradually beginning to understand. Well-known neuroscientist Paul Zak and author of the book *The Moral Molecule: the Source of Love and Prosperity*, discovered through his research that stories which succeed in bringing out the emotional connect release oxytocin, a hormone secreted by the pituitary gland, a small pea-sized structure at the base of the brain. This hormone also goes by the name of 'cuddle hormone' because it is released when people snuggle up or bond socially; some even call it the 'love hormone' because of its role in forging human connections, and creating empathy.

In a 2014 *HBR* article about his work, Zak stated that when stories follow a certain pattern, which includes first developing and then sustaining engagement and tension, basically ensuring that people eventually become strongly invested in the outcome, a strong emotional connection forms between the audience and storyteller.

So very strong is that connection that the audience almost literally starts experiencing the emotions of the storyteller and the 'love hormone' oxytocin hormone is released. The release of the hormone is itself significant, for once released, it helps make the listeners trust the person narrating the story and take whatever action the storyteller asks them to take.

Remember, people buy from emotions and justify with logic. It is never the other way round. Unfortunately, most people or marketers believe they can convince the consumer to buy using data and logic; and then hope the consumer will develop an emotional connect with the brand. This is merely fanciful thinking. In reality, establishing the emotional connect comes first; logic is what the consumer himself uses to explain or justify how he feels about the product.

BEING AN EFFECTIVE STORYTELLER

Here are some guidelines to those of you who wish to tell an effective story:

It is important to tell the audience what makes the story special. This can be how your story changed you or the course of your life. Stories must take the audience on a journey of transformation; else they are just anecdotes. Some call this the 'aha' moment, the point when it all begins to make sense to the audience, when they associate completely with what happens to the narrator.

Stories must focus on the human element. People are not interested during the story to hear the facts of the situation. They wish to know what you did or how you reacted in a particular situation. Remember the words of Maya Angelou, the famous American poet, singer and civil rights activist. She said, 'People will forget what you said, people will forget what you did, but people will never forget how you made them feel.' It is the 'feeling' element that must be strongly projected in the story. Take your audience through your pains and tribulations, feelings of hope and despair, happiness and celebration.

One more example from Google's advertising campaigns illustrates this best. Watch their 'Reunion' advertisement. It is a wonderful example of telling a story that hits you hard, and once again, the brand is kept in the background.

The advertisement commences with an old man in India speaking to his granddaughter about a childhood friend from across the border; he and his friend haven't seen each other since India and Pakistan became separate countries. The granddaughter is moved by the story and uses Google's various services to ultimately track down the friend and arrange a reunion on the occasion of the old man's birthday. The gentle pathos and strong narrative is incredible.

Finally, the story must have a clear meaning. As mentioned above, it must take the audience from the specific to the universal. Think of the stories in the *Panchatantra* or *Aesop's Fables*. They all have a clear meaning or moral. They take the audience through what happens to a specific individual to make a point in the nature of a revelation. This can be about human nature or how people should behave or act.

Religious teachers understood this well. Look at the number of analogies, parables and stories they often tell. They tell good stories and leave it to the audience to make their conclusions on what constitutes good or bad behaviour, right and wrong. The Jataka Tales, the parable of the Good Samaritan, etc., reflect this technique.

Hence, remember that when you finish your story and the final line is said, the audience should know exactly why they took the journey with you.

This aspect of the meaning is perhaps the most important. Nancy Duarte is a well-known American writer and speaker. Being the author of several books, including *Slide:ology: The Art and Science of Creating Great Presentations* (2008), *Resonate: Present Visual Stories that Transform Audiences* (2010), *HBR Guide to Persuasive Presentations* (2012) and *Illuminate: Ignite Change through Speeches, Stories, Ceremonies and Symbols* (2016), she calls this to be the 'STAR moment', STAR standing for 'Something to Always Remember'. Make sure you know what message you want your audience to leave with.

'MAKE IT FASCINATING'

Stories are the best way to drive commitment or to get people to change, overcome assumptions, biases and prejudices. They can often succeed where data and logic cannot for they appeal to people's feelings and emotions, often lifting them from the challenges of day-to-day routines to a higher cause. In effect, stories can help change people's view of the world and the lens with which they consider things.

Corporates have often tapped into the art of storytelling to ensure that the consumer remains emotionally connected and invested in their brand. AirBnB, a well-known company, which runs a platform for users to list, discover and book accommodations during their travel, has space on its website for users to recount and publish their stories, based on their unique travel experiences. As David Ogilvy, the advertising tycoon and founder of advertising agency Ogilvy & Mather (O&M), who was called the 'Father of Advertising', had said, 'Tell the truth, but make it fascinating'.

Chapter 10

What's Your Purpose in the World?

Simon Sinek has achieved worldwide fame through his books and TED talks on 'Finding Your Why'. In the beginning of the book, this is what he writes:[1]

> The goal of this book is not simply to try to fix the things that aren't working. Rather, I wrote this book as a guide to focus on and amplify the things that do work. The stories that follow are of those individuals and organizations that naturally embody this pattern. They are the ones that start with Why.

Sinek goes on to give examples of leaders such as Martin Luther King inventors such as the Wright brothers and personalities such as Steve Jobs to illustrate how great leaders inspire communicating 'Why' they do things.

The author says that most companies sell their products or service focusing on the 'What' that the products and services do, stating they have launched a new product or service or something on these lines. Next, the companies move on to the 'how': how the product is better or how they have made it—'using artificial intelligence', 'detergent with micro granules', 'cars with leather seats', all being examples that I have heard on television in India for actual products.

Finally, companies put out a call to action: 'book your test drive', 'order today for 20 per cent discount' being examples here that all readers will be familiar with, having often heard these concepts.

However, people do not really associate with companies or develop a loyalty towards its products or services because of the 'what' and the 'how'. Most companies that have been successful is because they have commanded a loyalty towards the 'purpose' which drives them.

---

[1] Simon Sinek, *Start with Why—How Great Leaders Inspire Everyone to Take Action* (Penguin Books, 2009).

Let us take the example of Indian companies. Many in India have a strong loyalty towards the Tata brand. What makes it so special? Let us look at its history. The Tata Group today is a conglomerate of nearly 100 companies encompassing several businesses across several business sectors: these include chemicals, consumer products, energy, engineering, information systems, materials and services.

But the firm had very modest beginnings, like many others. The Tata Group was founded as a private trading firm in 1868 by the entrepreneur and philanthropist Jamsetji Nusserwanji Tata. In 1902, the group incorporated the Indian Hotels Company to commission the Taj Mahal Palace and Tower, which was the first luxury hotel in India. After the pioneer Jamsetji Tata's passing away, in 1904, his son Sir Dorabji Tata took over as chairman, leading to diversifications into sectors such as steel, education, consumer goods and civil aviation (1932). The Tata Group started India's very first airline.

Later on, Jehangir Ratanji Dadabhoy Tata (J.R.D.) took over the as the Group chairman, further leading the company into even more sectors. It was one of the first Indian companies to get into software, and in 1945, the Group established the Tata Engineering and Locomotive Company (TELCO) to manufacture engineering and locomotive products; which was renamed as Tata Motors in 2003.

What holds the Group together? Many point to the legacy of the founder. In an era when there were few Indian or Indian-owned businesses, the patriarchs had the guts and gumption to establish a luxury hotel and steel company for the first time in the country. Their successors went on to run India's first airline, help the country make software, etc. There was always a strong sense of purpose in the Group, whose values included national building and philanthropy. This has also meant that the Trusts run by the Group have done much work in the social space; and the Group has established many institutions across the country which are well known for the research and work they do.

It is said that Jamsetji Tata had four ambitions; he wished to establish an iron and steel company, a unique hotel, a world-class learning institution and a hydro-electric plant. No doubt had he lived in a time when aviation was common that would have also been part of his goals, but the Wright brothers performed their famous flight only in 1903, just a year before Jamsetji passed away. However, the patriarch was able to realize his dream of a world-class hotel, with the Taj Hotel opening its doors in 1903.

So strong was the sense of purpose that his remaining ambitions were realized by subsequent Tata chairmen. The Tata Iron and Steel Company (TISCO), now known as Tata Steel, was established in 1907. Tata Power, established a hydro-electric plant a couple of years later. Finally, the Indian Institute of Science was established in 1911.

Contrast this with many other Indian corporates. Having worked with some of them, and having advised many as a consultant sometime in my career, I have often seen that they have been opportunistic, taking the plunge into whichever sector has been the 'flavour of the season' or which has offered them the opportunity to leverage some political connection or exploit some opportunity for monetary gain.

All these attempts have lacked true 'purpose', one may say the only real purpose was to make a pecuniary profit. This has meant that the company, while perhaps making short term gains, has not been able to succeed with its efforts for long.

This manifested itself in a number of Indian conglomerates jumping onto the infrastructure bandwagon at some time or the other. Many companies diversified into making roads or establishing power plants primarily because they felt they could extract a form of 'rent' by getting access to cheap raw material sources (in the case of power plants, this was either coal or natural gas) by signing agreements with Indian public sector entities; or get concessions to establish and collect tolls from the roads. This also manifested itself in the real estate sector, with many companies seeking to get their hands on lucrative land banks across the country.

Many of these projects—roads, power plants, real estate projects have never been completed. In many cases, the problem was most acute in the real estate segment where buyers had invested their hard-earned savings or taken loans from banks and had to pay Equated Monthly Instalments (EMIs) without gaining possession of the houses they had paid for. Many of these companies, which had become some of the largest in the country at one time, today have gone bankrupt or closed down. They have also affected their financers, notably banks, which are even today saddled with a relatively high amount of Non-Performing Assets (NPAs), in turn attracting worldwide scrutiny and forcing the Indian Government to intervene many a time.

All these efforts can be traced back to the fundamental issue that there was no real 'purpose' behind these diversifications. These companies had little genuine reason to get into new sectors, except being able to lay their hands on licenses, concessions or agreements by hook or by crook. Where has this seemingly initial benefit through 'connections' landed them today? Many businessmen have had to flee the country, either voluntary or after being served with notices by some regulatory authority or the other to settle their dues. All these businessmen and their businesses were motivated by greed or put more gently, by the possibility of short-term benefit, but lacked real purpose.

Hence, companies (and even people) in India would do well to ponder over their real purpose, before jumping on to the diversification bandwagon.

PATANJALI'S PURPOSE

Acharya Balkrishna and Baba Ramdev started their FMCG and Ayurvedic formulations' journey in 1990, when they set up the Divya Yog Pharmacy Trust. The trust at the time conducted yoga camps across the country and also sold Ayurvedic medicines at these camps.

From a ₹400 crore business in 2011, Patanjali today has a turnover in excess of ₹10,000 crore; demonstrating a near unbelievable rate of growth in excess of 100 per cent in many of these years; with products ranging from Ayurvedic medicines to personal care products and food. The company, its founders and its products have all become household names. The company can be easily termed as the biggest disruptor in the Indian FMCG industry.

It certainly made the traditional FMCG firms, be it Hindustan Unilever Ltd (HUL), P&G, Dabur, ITC, etc., sit up and take notice. By offering products that were notably cheaper than those sold by the aforesaid firms, Patanjali forced them in some cases to hold or even cut prices and also strengthen their product portfolios, especially in the naturals/ayurvedic space.

What was noteworthy about this company and worrisome for the MNC giants is that Patanjali directly attacked them, asking the Indian consumer that why should he/she purchase products from multinationals (MNCs) at a price higher than what the Indian firm could offer them, while matching its quality with that provided by the MNCs.

The FMCG space in India remains huge—it is USD 50 billion industry. Before the entry of Patanjali, it was dominated almost wholly by MNCs (with the possible exception of Dabur)- the top firms being Hindustan Unilever Ltd, P&G, Nestle, Colgate–Palmolive, Johnson & Johnson, etc.

What worked for Patanjali? Something certainly did, for an American business magazine ranked Baba Ramdev 27th in its list of 'Most Creative Business People of 2016', while his associate and current CEO of Patanjali Ayurved Acharya Balkrishna has made his debut on the *Forbes* list of India's 100 Richest People; given his ownership of ~95 per cent equity in the company.

It is also worth noting that other Indian companies, including Dabur, had for long used the Ayurvedic platform. Many of us will remember Dabur's 'Chyawanprash' with the image of an Indian rishi, toothpaste brands such as Meswak, etc.

In fact, both the Indian firm Dabur as well as the US MNC Coca-Cola were started in the mid-1880s (in the case of Dabur, it was Dr S. K. Burman, an Ayurvedic practitioner in Kolkata, who concocted medicines for diseases such as cholera and malaria and went on to set up Dabur India Ltd in 1884 to mass-produce his Ayurvedic formulations). But in all these intervening decades, Coca-Cola has become perhaps the best known brand in the world, present in almost every country across the globe and where does Dabur stand in comparison? Why? What are the reasons for the stark difference in the overall turnover? This is something worth thinking over.

So what did Patanjali do which other's didn't? How did this firm manage to succeed in challenging the might of the multinationals and in more than one case, overtake them in terms of sales? There are probably several sides to the story, but one aspect stands out, Patanjali got its purpose right.

Baba Ramdev, the brand ambassador and face of Patanjali embodied this sense of purpose almost in true letter and spirit. His discourses and yoga asanas succeeded in communicating an image of health and wellness that the products would bring. The Baba was clear in his communication of the purpose—buy our products because we are an Indian firm that produces healthy Ayurvedic products. Why buy the same products from MNCs that have many chemicals or synthetic ingredients?

At the end, Patanjali products were able to differentiate itself using a combination of Ayurveda and technology. The marketing was consistent—the products are culturally indigenous and the brand is totally 'Indian'.

Patanjali's growth story has been discussed both in Boardrooms as well as it has become a case study at management schools. This is a home-grown example of how starting with a sense of purpose, it has made so much of a difference.

BRANDS THAT HAVE FOUND THEIR 'PURPOSE'

There are many other brands that also embody the sense of purpose, which makes them stand out in the minds of consumers. One of these is the firm Chipotle, which says that it is in the business of good food. It seeks to use high quality raw ingredients, classic cooking techniques and distinctive interior design to bring elements of fine dining to quick service restaurants. At the same time, Chipotle also says it seeks to cultivate a better world with respect for animals, farmers and the environment. In short, it tries to be a 'food brand with integrity'.

Though the brand has faced some troubles of late, its founder Steve Ells has instituted an enhanced food safety plan that 'will establish Chipotle as an industry leader in food safety'.

Uber is also an example of finding and communicating a sense of purpose. The company says it is evolving the way the world moves. Its earlier mission statement reflected this, stating that its mission was to 'Make transportation as reliable as running water, everywhere, for everyone'. This was more recently changed to 'We ignite opportunity by setting the world in motion.'

And how does it do this? 'By seamlessly connecting riders to drivers through our apps, we make cities more accessible, opening up more possibilities for riders and more business for drivers.'

The brand succeeded in communicating its purpose. It has revolutionized the transportation segment in many countries; and is set to continue creating disruptions as it now tries out driverless vehicles and offer more services such as Uber Eats.

Similar to Uber, with its zero-inventory but high customer convenience model is Airbnb. The company says that it is a trusted community marketplace for consumers to list, discover and book unique accommodations for unique travel experiences.

Its mission is to help create a world where you can belong anywhere and where people can live in a place, instead of just traveling to it. In short, it offers a kind of home away from home. Put in another way, you can make your home (at least temporarily) in more than 34,000 cities and 190 countries using its platform.

Armour found its 'Why' by wishing to make all athletes better through passion, design and the relentless pursuit of innovation. It calls itself the originator of performance apparel, or athletic gear designed to keep athletes 'cool, dry and light throughout the course of a game, practice or workout'.

Many say that the U in UA (short for Under Armour) could well stand for 'Underdog' given the brand competes with global giants like Nike, Reebok, etc. But the little company solved a unique problem and also perfected its voice and how to communicate with its legion of devotees.

Virgin America said its mission is to make flying good again, with innovative features, new planes, attractive fares, top-notch service and a host of other amenities that reinvented domestic air travel.

'The Virgin America experience is unlike any other in the skies, featuring mood-lit cabins with WiFi, custom-designed leather seats, power outlets and a video touch-screen at every seat-back offering guests on-demand menus and countless entertainment options,' the brand adds. Its innovations included an integration with Google Street View that allows consumers to tour plane cabins, as well as a partnership with Netflix, which enables passengers to stream content in flight.

Virgin America addressed the issues of boring domestic air travel in the United States, its measures included a catchy in-flight safety video to making a video replicating the experience of flying on other airlines.

GANDHIAN LEADERSHIP AND THE 'PURPOSE'

The concept of Finding Your Purpose is important to leaders as much as companies. Mahatma Gandhi was one such individual who came to be called the 'Father of the Nation' because his 'why' was so clear. He would oppose what was unjust because it was morally wrong while staying close to his principles of truth and non-violence or 'satyagraha'.

The Dandi March is one such example. Conventionally, we say that following the law is moral; and breaking the law is not so. But the Mahatma was able to convince others that in this case, breaking the law was the moral or right thing to do, because the law itself was unjust.

The historic trial of Mahatma Gandhi in 1922 best illustrated Gandhi's 'Why'. The Mahatma was charged under Section 124 A of the Indian Penal Code, the offences being for his writings in three articles published in *Young India* of September 29 and December 15 of 1921, and February 23 of 1922. The offending articles were called 'Tampering with Loyalty'; 'The Puzzle and its Solution', and 'Shaking the Manes'.

The Mahatma pleaded guilty to the charges but stated that he wished to make a statement. He declared that he, once a supporter of the British, was now convinced that British rule was to be opposed because of what it had done to India and her people. He spoke about how he had been shocked and surprised by the Rowlatt Act, the Jallianwala Bagh massacre and other such occurrences.

The Mahatma stated:

> No sophistry, no jugglery in figures, can explain away the evidence that the skeletons in many villages present to the naked eye. I have no doubt whatsoever that both England and the town dwellers of India will have to answer, if there is a God above, for this crime against humanity, which is perhaps unequalled in history. The law itself in this country has been used to serve the foreign exploiter.
>
> My unbiased examination of the Punjab Martial law cases has led me to believe that at least 95 per cent of convictions were wholly bad. My experience of political cases in India leads me to the conclusion, in nine out of every ten, the condemned men were totally innocent. Their crime consisted in the love of their country.

In 99 cases out of hundred, justice has been denied to Indians as against Europeans in the courts of India. This is not an exaggerated picture. It is the experience of almost every Indian who has had anything to do with such cases. In my opinion, the administration of the law is thus prostituted, consciously or unconsciously, for the benefit of the exploiter.

He ended by telling the judge to give him the 'highest punishment' that the law provided, saying,

I am, therefore, here to submit not to a light penalty but to the highest penalty. I do not ask for mercy. I do not plead any extenuating act. I am here, therefore, to invite and cheerfully submit to the highest penalty that can be inflicted upon me for what in law is a deliberate crime, and what appears to me to be the highest duty of a citizen. The only course open to you, the Judge, is, as I am going to say in my statement, either to resign your post, or inflict on me the severest penalty if you believe that the system and law you are assisting to administer are good for the people.

So eloquent and passionate was the Mahatma's statement that on its completion, even as the judge cited the court trial of Lokmanya Tilak, and based on the same ruling announced six years of imprisonment to Gandhi, he added, 'Nobody would be happier than me the day the government releases you from the prison'; and going on to say, 'You are in a different category from any person I have ever tried or am likely ever to try...in the eyes of millions of your countrymen you are a great patriot and a great leader; even all those who differ from you in politics look up to you as a man of high ideals and of noble and even saintly life.[2]'

---

[2] *Selected Works of Mahatma Gandhi*, Vol. VI.

Millions followed the Mahatma and many were even willing to lay down their lives not because of his great oratory or play with words, but because they were convinced that the reason he was doing what he was doing; his 'Why' was moral and just. The small frail man 'in a loincloth', the 'half-naked fakir' as Churchill once described him shook the foundations of the British empire because his 'Why' was so powerful.

Many other leaders who followed the Mahatma's footsteps such as Martin Luther King in the United States, Nelson Mandela in South Africa also found strength in their purpose. In both cases, their 'purpose' was fighting an unjust system that discriminated against people based on their colour or racial background. Nelson Mandela once said, 'I hate race discrimination most intensely and in all its manifestations. I have fought it all during my life; I fight it now, and will do so until the end of my days.' Their cause was just; as the wise saying goes: 'Thrice is he armed who hath his quarrel just'.

FIND AND COMMUNICATE YOUR PURPOSE

The examples covered in this chapter, both of great companies and great leaders, point to the need for every company to understand and communicate their purpose.

People do indeed want good products or great service; but often and this is also very important -they have a marked preference for people and companies they respect, trust and admire.

It is therefore important for a customer to know a little bit about you or your company; your story and why you do what you do. Let us consider a prospective customer who has visited your website, retail store or any other place where he can make purchase.

Try and make sure you get a message across about your company. What is it that would inspire a consumer to want to start a relationship with you? Can you communicate this in a succinct but attractive manner? You will find this goes a long way in making the sale.

As we pointed out earlier, there is one thing not even your biggest competitor can steal from you—and that is 'Your Purpose'.

Chapter 11

The Threes Have It!

There is a Latin phrase 'omnetrium perfectum'. This means that everything that comes in threes is perfect, or put slightly differently, everything coming in a set of three is complete.

In my corporate life so far, I have had many occasion to mull on the 'power of three'. Famous words, slogans, film titles, even titles of stories for children and a variety of other things have been structured in threes. Similarly, adjectives are often grouped in threes to emphasize an idea.

Let us consider some famous examples of this grouping:

- Story Titles
  o The Three Little Pigs
  o Three Billy Goats Gruff
  o Three Musketeers
  o Goldilocks and the Three Bears
  o The Three Stooges
- From Religion
  o The Holy Trinity—in the name of the father, the son and the holy spirits
  o The three stages of life—birth, death and rebirth
  o Body, mind and spirit
  o The Three Wise Men
- Famous Quotes and Speeches
  o 'Friends, Romans, Countrymen, lend me your ears'
  o Julius Caesar's 'Veni, vidi, vici': 'I came, I saw, I conquered'
  o 'Life, liberty, and the pursuit of happiness'

- o 'Government of the people, by the people, for the people'

- o 'Blood, sweat, and tears'

- o 'Location, location, location'

- o 'Faith, hope, and charity'

- o 'Mind, body, spirit'

- o 'Stop, look and listen'

- o Our priorities are 'Education, Education, Education'

- o 'Duty—Honour—Country. Those three hallowed words reverently dictate what you ought to be, what you can be, and what you will be'

- o That's the truth, the whole truth, and nothing but the truth

In corporate life, I have often found that making points in threes is so much more effective than doing so in twos or fours. This has been supported by much empirical research. Why is it so?

The concept is well known; and termed as 'The Rule of Three'. It works due to the presence of the writer being able to generate concise, memorable patterns. In addition, it appears that human beings are preconditioned to respond favourably to elements grouped in threes.

It relates to the way we humans process information. We have become proficient at pattern recognition by necessity, and three is the smallest and most effective number of elements required to create a pattern.

This combination of pattern plus brevity results in memorable content, and that's why the Rule of Three works! If you want something stuck in someone's head and use it to convince them, put it in a sequence of three. By repeating something three times or using alliteration with three words, a relatively ordinary set of points becomes more memorable or emotive.

PUTTING THE THREES TO WORK

In case you are making a speech and want your message to be remembered, put it into a list of three. Let us consider political slogans for example which parties want to strike a chord with:

- *Ma, Maati, Maanush*
- *Ram, Roti, Ekta*

Or even the Olympic motto: Citius, Altus, Fortus (Higher, Faster, Stronger); the motto of the French Revolution: 'Liberty, Equality, Fraternity'; and Nike's slogan: 'Just Do It'.

On the other hand, if you are making a PowerPoint presentation, use no more than three themes per slide. If you are using the storytelling approach, try and use the Rule of Three. The story works its way into the reader's head through repetition of part of the story. The first two times build tension, and the third releases the tension, either through the resolution of the plot or a twist in the narrative.

As mentioned above, traditional folktales have this structure all through them. Many plays today also use the 'three act sequence' and most stories have three parts—the beginning, middle and end.

Now let us assume you have to market your product or service. The Rule of Three is one of the best ways you can speak about the product. Limit your communication to three important points about your product or service. If it is more than three, one seems to lose the consumer's attention as he/she might think that you are placing before him/her a laundry list of product features. Any less than three and it's not enough to convince him or her to make the purchase. Remember the Latin saying: 'Three is perfect' and 'Three is complete'.

Before making a purchase, especially one that has a relatively high degree of 'involvement', consumers indulge in comparison. They may compare benefits, features, prices. Very likely they will compare based on three parameters; more than three is unlikely for the consumer may not have sufficient information. I would venture to suggest that if you can score on at least three points or provide three reasons for the customer to mentally justify his/her purchase, you will make the sale.

Very often, while framing strategy, I have found myself in a situation where I have to make recommendations. In the early part of my career, I made the mistake of listing down all possible things that could be done, making a laundry list of sorts. I was often surprised, but despite my being so comprehensive with my recommendations and covering all possible solutions and angles, it never seemed to inspire people to take the next step.

Gradually, I learnt that the art of effective presentation and convincing people lay in saying what was just enough-no more and no less. Outlining too many possibilities and possible courses of action often backfired. It intimidated people as there were too many choices. My bosses felt more analysis was needed before deciding on the next steps.

Now, I do not make laundry lists. I conduct rigorous analysis before my presentation, eliminating choices that I feel are not prudent. When I outline possibilities, I say I have narrowed down the options to three—as that seem the most practical. I then discuss the pros and cons of these final three options.

While I do not succeed every time, my success rate with convincing people has vastly improved! It seems 'three options' are much easier for people to mentally grasp and wrestle with and make a decision.

Listing these three means that I have done my homework, eliminating points just for the sake of adding them. Since I have listed just three points, I have a very strong rationale why they are there in the first place.

I have extended this use of 'Threes' to almost all my communication. When I have to list strengths or weaknesses of a product or any entity, I focus on the top three points. The top three after all, are the key strengths.

USING THE RULE OF THREE

I would strongly advise that we look to use this concept in our communications. How can we do so in presentations?

Remember, the audience, in all likelihood, will remember only three things from your presentation; so plan in advance what these will be. Effective presentations mean that the audience should take away exactly what you wish them to, neither less nor more than what you desire.

- **Before you start writing your presentation, plan your three key messages.** Once you have the three messages, structure the main part of your presentation around these three key themes. Now decide how you would like to embellish these points—you may use videos or graphics, etc. But don't let the audience forget the three main points!

So when you wish to talk about your product or service, let the presentation have three benefits of using it. As an example, if you were talking about the technical features of the product, you could speak about how it offers the following:

o   Increased speed

o   Increased size

o   More storage

Then, you could add details to buttress your points.

In 2011, Apple's Steve Jobs introduced the iPad 2 as being 'thinner, lighter, and faster' than the original. The three adjectives so accurately described the new device, many hundred headlines and blogs used the same three words. It was a great example of how Jobs had used his communication style to get exactly the result he wanted.

You could also ensure that there are three parts to your presentation. More matter might make the audience feel that you are trying to do too much or that the presentation is too long. So stick to these three—the beginning, the middle and the end. Plan what you will do in these three parts. Use the beginning, for example, for an attention grabber (could be some eye-catching statistic) or for an ice breaker.

- **Use lists of three wherever you can in your presentation.** As mentioned earlier, keep your number of points to three; and limit each slide to containing a maximum of three points. Too many points are intimidating. Do your analysis and leave out what is not vital. Remember that 'Less is More'.

I would go so far as to say that if you have four points to get across, cut out one; or club it with another to get the final list to three. Few will remember the fourth point anyway. It will be redundant. You will see the difference that an effective use of this rule makes. Follow the Rule of Three to ensure your points are pithy, concise and effective!

STRUCTURING PRESENTATIONS USING THE RULE OF THREE

How do you best structure your presentation to ensure the audience retains what you wish to say? Dale Carnegie once provided some very good advice. He said whenever you are trying to communicate something, 'Tell them what you are going to tell them, tell them, then tell them what you just told them.'

What does this practically entail?

It means that always provide a preview to the audience first before you launch into the content of your speech or presentation. This 'preview' can simply be a succinct Table of Contents or something on these lines.

Next, you must have your main content. This must ideally have three major points or ideas, which you back with examples, data or statistics. One way to narrate an effective story using the Rule of Three is to think of three adjectives related to your main points and then tell stories that are examples of those adjectives.

Finally, you have a summary. "Tell them what you just told them," as Carnegie said. Sometimes this is important to ensure that your audience doesn't forget your key messages, or are not misinterpreted.

Let us look at one great example of how this Rule of Three was used effectively in a speech—this comes from the great Civil Rights leader, Martin Luther King. Look how he ends using the rule so magnificently to bring the audience to its feet:

> I say to you today, my friends, that in spite of the difficulties and frustrations of the moment I still have a dream. It is a dream deeply rooted in the American dream.

> I have a dream that one day this nation will rise up and live out the true meaning of its creed: "We hold these truths to be self – evident; that all men are created equal.

> I have a dream that one day on the red hills of Georgia the sons of former slaves and the sons of former slave owners will be able to sit down together at the table of brotherhood.

> I have a dream that one day even the state of Mississippi, a desert state sweltering in the heat of injustice and oppression, will be transformed into an oasis of freedom and justice.

> I have a dream that my four little children will one day live in a nation where they will not be judged by the colour of their skin but by the content of their character.

> I have a dream today.

> I have a dream that one day the state of Alabama, whose governor's lips are presently dripping with the words of interposition and nullification, will be transformed into a situation where little black boys and black girls will be able to join hands with little white boys and white girls and walk together as sisters and brothers.

> I have a dream today.

> When we let freedom ring, when we let it ring from every village and every hamlet, from every state and

every city, we will be able to speed up that day when all of God's children, black men and white men, Jews and Gentiles, Protestants and Catholics, will be able to join hands and sing in the words of the old Negro spiritual, 'Free at last! Free at last! Thank God Almighty, we are free at last!'

Chapter 12

Arise, Awake and Start-up!

Arise, awake and stop not till the goal is reached.

—Swami Vivekananda

I have had the occasion to work with many start-up firms over the past few years as a mentor and guide; these start-ups are being based in the United States, Israel and of course, India. In this chapter, I would like to share a few aspects that I feel start-ups should keep in mind and also some resources that would likely be of benefit to start-up entities across different sectors.

STARTING YOUR START-UP

One crucial upfront matter for the start-up is to get a fix on the following matters:

- Whom is your product or service meant for and what problem is your product or service trying to solve?

- Is your potential target audience big enough, or if you are wishing to operate in a niche, is it profitable enough? Hence, what are the potential sales from your idea?

- Are there any alternative means to solve the same problem?

- What makes your idea so special?

- Can you show your idea clearly to others? Will they latch on and back it?

- Who do you need to make your idea work?

- What do you need to make your start-up work?

- Is your start-up scalable? Can you grow your business within the timeframe that your potential investors might desire?

- Can you make your start-up successful with your extant set of skills?

I would suggest that anyone starting his company gets a fix on each of these questions and outlines the answers clearly. Indeed, this should be part of the pitch made to anyone external for support, be it funding or otherwise.

Many start-up companies begin with an idea that has its roots in some personal experience or frustration. But the crucial matter is that whether the solution you have based your company is scalable and if you have validated it, therefore, with an audience that extends beyond your immediate circle of family and friends.

This is where robust research comes in. Definitely do a lot of quantitative research, which can take the form of surveys and data collection. For this, try and limit audience response to questions around frequency of use and simple 'Yes', and 'No'-type answers. These give you unambiguous feedback and are less subject to your optimism in interpretation. The optimism bias is something that sinks most start-up companies for they tend to interpret results in ways that justify their business, rather than look at data in an objective way. Hence, do perform quantitative surveys with such simple questions.

Once you know your idea is on a sound footing and data indicates you have a market, then use qualitative surveys. This helps to provide depth of understanding; it can be of the consumer's usage habits, his way of consuming, his preferences, etc. It also helps you to fine tune your solution to match consumer tastes.

An important aspect today is to build 'user personas'. This refers to the habits, tastes and features of your user. What does he/she like? How does he/she consume? Where does he/she consume? Personas are important to define the basic features and desired user experience for your product.

Use the following resources in your journey:

- Spend time with the 'Start up school' series by Y Combinator (it is on YouTube and features many different speakers and topics)

- Study Y Combinator Paul Graham's essays. He covers many aspects including how to access funding, building pitch decks, etc.

- Look through some of the books of Eric Ries on start-ups. The Lean Start-up is a well-known publication of his.

- For surveys use free resources as much as possible; Survey Monkey, for example, provides the ability to create surveys to obtain feedback or design questionnaires

- If you are a tech start-up, you must understand the basics of the tech that you offer. Free (and paid) courses are available today from providers like Udemy, Coursera, etc. Look through resources available through Massive Open Online Courseware (MOOCs).

- Sign up for newsletters that provide content or information in the area your start-up operates in.

- Industry data is available through Euromonitor, Nielsen; and resources such as Mary Meeker's Internet Trends, etc.

- You can build your own website in little time. I often tell my students to use free or inexpensive resources such as Wix or Sitebuilder

- Obtain analytics of website traffic from resources such as Google Analytics and others; LinkedIn also offers this for your LinkedIn page

- Prototyping tools include Invision, Origami, etc., these generally have free trial versions.

- Finally, speak to other start-ups and find a good mentor. Be willing to part with equity if needed to get a good mentor on board. Other start-ups can provide you with valuable tips as they have been there, done that.

THE MACRO VIEW

The view from the balcony appears very different from that people, who are 'playing the game', have in the field. In large organizations, there are often different people who 'sit on the balcony' and those who are 'playing the game'.

When you are commencing your journey, however, you have to have the skills to take the balcony view as well as that of the captain in the field.

You will need to understand your industry well. What is the size of the industry, its growth rate, the key players, etc.? Where is the industry heading towards? What are the trends? For example, are we moving towards disintermediation? If so, there is little point in becoming an intermediary. Are we moving towards greater personalization? If so, does your idea contain the ability to personalize content or other aspects for the user?

GET STARTED QUICKLY

It is important to get started. I strongly suggest to get your product, your service or offering into the market quickly and obtain the initial user feedback. This is what 'beta versions' are for. Don't wait to try to come up with something perfect in every manner, for there will always be some changes that you need to make; something unforeseen that you will need to address.

In the words of Donald Rumsfield, there will always be some 'unknown unknowns'. To make these known, you have to get your product into the market.

After launching, measure incessantly. 'What cannot be measured cannot be managed' is an old adage. Paul Graham, the English-born computer scientist, entrepreneur, venture capitalist, author, and essayist, who is perhaps best known for co-founding the influential start-up accelerator and seed capital firm Y Combinator, puts it well[1]:

> You make what you measure.... Merely measuring something has an uncanny tendency to improve it. If you want to make your user numbers go up, put a big piece of paper on your wall and every day plot the number of users. You'll be delighted when it goes up and disappointed when it goes down. Pretty soon you'll start noticing what makes the number go up, and you'll start to do more of that.

The basic tenet is to get an understanding quickly of what works in the market and what doesn't.

Remember that sometimes the most successful products are not the best or cheapest, but they offer one compelling benefit that helps it stand out from others. Think Steve Jobs when he launched the Apple iPod with the line, 'a thousand songs in your pocket'. The fact that music aficionados did not have to now carry around many Compact Discs (CDs) or other gadgets but could access their entire music library with such a small gadget made it a winner.

So, if you want to make cakes and sell them online, start with preparing them at home and offering them for delivery

---

[1] Paul Graham, 'Startups in 13 sentences'; http://paulgraham.com/13sentences.html.

at least in your neighbourhood or nearby colonies. Think of what all you will learn:

- What ingredients people prefer
- What time of day they usually order
- What price points work
- What promotions people like
- What kind of add-ons people wish for
- How to manage your inventory
- How to manage delivery
- Whether home delivery adds much value
- How to manage your resources
- Whether your costs are similar or more than what you budgeted for, etc.

Eric Ries makes the point of going to market early in his book *The Lean Start up: How Today's Entrepreneurs Use Continuous Innovation to Create Radically Successful Businesses*. He attributes the failure of his first venture to spending too much time and effort trying to perfect his initial product and its launch.

He says he made the mistake of working forward from the technology he had developed; rather than taking the business results he wanted to achieve and working backwards from that. He says it is important to start by interviewing and understanding customers, and working from that to build a solution that meets their needs. In his book, he talks about building an MVP (Minimum Viable Product) and then testing and iterating quickly. This is akin to a lean manufacturing set-up since it results in less waste and a better product market fit. Ries also recommends using Taiichi Ohno's approach of 'the Five Whys', a technique designed to reach the root cause of an issue.

The term Minimum Viable Product, referring to a product or service with just enough features to satisfy early customers and provide feedback for further iterations was coined by Frank Robinson, but popularized by Ries. One of the benefits of building this and going to market is that it helps bust any assumptions (or ego) that the founders may have had. Ries states that the MVP is that 'version of a new product that a team uses to collect the maximum amount of validated learning about customers with the least effort.'

VALUATION OF START-UPS

I have often been asked as to which method I prefer while valuing start-ups. Many start-up entities also wish to know how angel investors or venture capitalists decide their valuation so that they can work accordingly to build this up and get a 'better deal'.

I generally prefer using either of the following two methods to arrive at a valuation; and will detail them here because they are not as well known in India as in the US or Europe:

- The eponymous Berkus Method
- The Scorecard method

Berkus Method

The Berkus Method basically looks at how start-ups have addressed common risks; and assigns a range of values to how well the start-up has done in addressing the risk. The more the risks addressed, the higher the valuation.

Now, one can say that the broad category of risks that start-ups face are the following:

- Having a good enough business idea
- The technology risk
- The market risk (including risk from competition)
- The risk in execution or implementation of the idea and the business plan
- The risks associated with actual production/operations

These risks can be addressed by various initiatives. Technology risk can be addressed by testing a prototype and checking whether the technology works. I was once advising a group of students who had a start-up that wished to offer battery-operated two-wheelers as a mobility solution for people to cover short distances. They clearly needed to ensure, amongst other things, that unscrupulous riders would not make off with the bike! So they had looked at a technology that could remotely disable the bike if its GPS co-ordinates indicated suspicious user activity. But this technology had to be tested. So, the first thing they were asked to do is show a prototype of their proposed mobility solution with the features that they wished to incorporate.

Similarly, execution risk can be addressed by ensuring quality in the management team. Indeed, the quality of the team, their credibility and experience is one of the most crucial determinants of valuation.

Market risks can be addressed through deep partnerships. Considering again the start-up that wished to provide a mobility solution, one of the areas I advised them to focus was on establishing partnerships. This could be with real estate firms that owned office complexes such as DLF, Unitech, etc., or mall owners. These partnerships could give them access to parking or charging infrastructure in areas of high footfall and where their target audience would be located.

So, to sum up, the following table provides a synopsis of the Berkus Method:

EXISTENCE OF THIS PARAMETER	VALUATION IT ADDS (MAX VALUATION)
Robust business idea	USD 500 million
Existence of a prototype	USD 500 million
The quality of management team	USD 500 million
Presence of strategic relationships	USD 500 million
Product rollout or sales	USD 500 million

This method was developed by the angel investor David Berkus. He found that looking at estimates of revenue that the start-ups provided hardly helped as the actual revenues were way off the estimates. In fact, according to Berkus, only 1 in 20 start-ups (or 5 per cent) actually meet revenue forecasts. So he developed this method that focused on key parameters which in effect, increased the likelihood or probability of success.

As the table indicates, the Berkus method indicates that the highest valuation a star-tup could get would be USD 2.5 million; and if it is still at the idea or concept stage, it would score USD 2 million. While some feel this method is relatively simplistic, it does provide a ready reckoner to assess early-stage start-ups.

Scorecard Method

A slightly more complex method was developed by Bill Payne, who was the Angel Capital Association's 2009 US

Angel Investor of the Year. He details the method in his book *The Definitive Guide to Raising Money from Angels*.

What is this method? It uses the average pre-money valuation of other seed/start-up businesses in the area, and then judges the particular start-up that needs to be evaluated, by comparing it against them, using a scorecard.

So we start by finding the average pre-money valuation of other pre-revenue companies in the geographic region and business sector of the start-up that is to be valued.

The scorecard method uses certain parameters as in the Berkus method; but gives different levels of importance to these as follows,

- Strength of the management team: 0–30 per cent

- Size of the opportunity: 0–25 per cent

- The product, service or technology that the start-up is advocating: 0–15 per cent

- The market or competitive environment: 0–10 per cent

- Marketing/sales channels/partnerships: 0–10 per cent

- Need for additional investment: 0–5 per cent

- Other parameters: The balance 0–5 per cent

As you can see, some of the parameters are similar to the Berkus method, and the quality and experience of the management team gets the highest importance.

Finally, we need to assign a factor to each of the above parameters based on the target start-up and then to multiply the sum of factors by the average pre-money valuation of pre-revenue companies. This Comparison Factors requires some strong sectoral research and understanding.

Let us take an example, similar to what the founder of this method used. For the sake of clarity, we will take simple numbers. Consider that most companies in the sector have strong teams, so the comparison factor for the management team is 100 per cent.

But suppose the start-up in question has some better technology than other companies, we can use a product technology comparison factor of 150 per cent.

We can use the following table assuming other such comparison factors:

COMPARISON FACTOR	WEIGHT %	COMPARISON %	FACTOR = (WXC)
Strength of entrepreneur and team	30	100	0.3000
Size of the opportunity	25	125	0.3125
Product/technology	15	150	0.2250
Competitive environment	10	80	0.0800
Marketing/sales/partnerships	10	100	0.1000
Need for additional investment	5	100	0.0500
Other factors (great location)	5	125	0.0625
SUM			1.1300

In the final step, we multiply the sum of the factors, here 1.13, by the average industry pre-revenue valuation of similar companies. Assuming this is USD 2 million, the start-up in question will be valued at 1.13 × 2 million = 2.26 million.

Basically, what we have done here is compare your target company to the norm (or average in the industry) for the chosen parameters. In the above table, we have evaluated the company's location as being 25 per cent better than those of its competitors, for example, hence, giving it a comparison factor of 125 per cent.

There is no sacrosanct number about the weights in this method as we are only comparing entities. So for example, if you wish to assign a higher weight to some parameter, you can go ahead in this system.

ADVICE TO START-UPS

I have been fortunate enough to interact with a number of start-ups. This is what I have learnt in terms of what separates the more successful ones from those that are less so:

A Good Co-founder Is a Must

Having a co-founder who is as passionate about you and as involved is important. Now this is tricky, for I have seen many start-ups that operate as a one-man show. If at all, there is a second partner, he is far less involved than the original founder. So do you need a partner at all?

The answer is that start-ups that are one-people shows will struggle to raise funding from external sources. Angel investors and Venture Capitalists (VCs) do feel that one founder is too less to run successful operations. There is also the additional risk—what if something was to happen to this one person? After all, it is the Angel investor or VC's funds at stake.

This risk is more pronounced when the start-up is run by a passionate student or someone just out of an engineering institute. What if the founder was to suddenly decide to seek a conventional corporate job and drop the start-up?

What if parental pressures were to force him to seek a more conventional job? This is why more external funding agencies will always like to see two or more closely involved in the business; along with a team below them.

If you do find a co-founder, make sure things are spelt out in black and white with legally valid documents. It is also useful to spell out each founder's areas of work clearly. For example, fund raising itself can be a full-time job; hence, it may be better that one founder devotes himself to this task, rather than both or all of the founders having to put in their time.

Don't Get Carried Away with Your Product or Offering

All of us at some time or the other have got carried away with something or the other. We have been too optimistic or over-enthusiastic and believed we have something that others will be keen to use, buy or have. Reality checks are important.

This is especially true with technology. Always remember to focus not on the tech itself, but the benefits that it brings to the user. You have developed something using AI at college? How does it change life for the user? Does it do something for him which he/she values? Or is it just gimmicky?

Focusing on the benefits of the offering, including in marketing communications, not just its technical features, is vital in determining success. Always get user feedback on whether the benefits are really a big deal.

Launch Early and Get Feedback

As I have said earlier in this chapter, it is better to launch quickly with a minimum viable product and it is vital to see user acceptance and feedback. 'Don't let the great be the enemy of the good,' while launching your new product or service. You will need to make iterations; so get it into the market soon and understand user feedback.

When you are considering the user feedback, remember what Paul Graham, co-founder of Y-Combinator, says: 'Ideally you want to make large numbers of users love you, but you can't expect to hit that right away. Initially you have to choose between satisfying all the needs of a subset of potential users, or satisfying a subset of the needs of all potential users. Take the first.'

What this means is that at least a few users love you by providing them 100 per cent satisfaction. Don't aim for just a 70 per cent score. If you have a new technology, the 'early adopters' must really feel that the new tech is wonderful, even if they are a small number in total. So a small number of people initially must really fall in love with your offering or service.

Financing

This is, of course, something that all start-ups look for sooner or later. You have to get the timing right, for financing does come with costs, including some dilution of control. So look for funding when you have a clear need for it; and don't look for more than you really need.

At the same time, going to professional angel investors and VCs provides a good reality check—do you have an idea and a product that others are willing to bet on and invest in?

Also, remember that nothing succeeds like success as far as financing is concerned. Often, you will find that possible funding individuals or entities do not wish to be the first to fund a start-up, but will jump on board if someone else commits first. This is a reality that all start-ups face.

I remember how difficult it was to find a publisher for my first book, but once I had my first book published by a reputed global publishing house, there were much fewer issues to find publishers for my subsequent books.

Scaling up

The ability to scale up is what all investors look for; for they are generally pretty aggressive when it comes to growth. So look to see how you can set up your firm with the inbuilt ability to scale up fairly rapidly.

As Paul Graham mentions, if students of one college could use Facebook (Harvard, in this case), there was no reason why those of other institutes and indeed, the whole world in general could not; on the other hand, if you have a juice parlour in one college, it is far from easy to extend it to 100 colleges for it brings far more challenges, including managing logistics of a perishable product, manpower, quality, etc.

Always Network

This is one thing you should never stop doing. Talk to as many people as possible, including your customers and users. Those who you keep in touch with could turn into important allies. 'Make connections and keep a record on each person you meet,' Clare Dreyer, a career expert, reportedly said. 'Ask for their advice and help. Keep in touch with them along the way and build your network before you need it! Quality relationships are the keys to the kingdom.'

Networking is also important because as an entrepreneur, you must always be a learner or student—willing to listen to others, their advice and their ideas; and of course, learn from those who have 'been there done that' before.

Resilience and Conviction

All the other points notwithstanding, the most crucial aspect is for the founder(s) of the start-up to have oodles of resilience and conviction. Ups and downs will always be there; but you really have to believe in yourself and your idea. This will also help you recruit or enlist others in your growth story.

Remember, that success ultimately depends on your motivation, drive and resilience. You will need to set the example for the rest of the team with your attitude, work ethic and determination.

Work Hard; Be Genuine and Establish Your Expertise

Being an entrepreneur is not easy. You have to work really hard; and above all be genuine. This takes many forms: it includes being a real expert in the industry where your firm chooses to play, understanding trends and knowing what others in the industry are doing.

So you have to 'establish your expertise'. The success of your business may well depend upon your reputation as an expert in the space that you are working in. It is only logical as few would want to buy anything from someone who possibly doesn't know what they are talking about.

So look for opportunities to establish your expertise; write blogs as well as articles for reputed publications; maintain a YouTube channel; speak at various fora; use podcasts; etc. this will help you gain trust of your customers and potential investors. Clicks, views of your podcasts, videos and other content all help establish your credentials.

Being genuine also means making or providing what your customer really needs- so you have to understand your customer really well. This means a lot of research and taking first-hand feedback. All this requires a lot of work. Never underestimate the work that you will have to put in.

Find Mentors

As you expand, you will need mentors and even perhaps an advisory board in place who can provide advice and guidance. Don't be afraid to ask people to mentor you; remember, they may have also risen to where they are due to the good advice they once received from mentors and guides!

Chapter 13

Being Bold

Do not go where the path may lead; but go where there is no path and leave a trail.

—Ralph Waldo Emerson

On 8 November 2016, the prime minister of India went live on national television and announced that his government was shortly withdrawing the usage of ₹500 and ₹1,000 denomination banknotes in the economy; this decision was subsequently termed as 'demonetization'. A new series of ₹500 and ₹2,000 banknotes were to be used; and all those who possessed the old series of notes (which was almost everyone in the country) were asked to deposit them by a certain date, for they would no longer constitute legal tender.

The prime minister claimed that the action would curtail the 'shadow' (or 'black') economy and reduce the use of illicit and counterfeit cash to fund illegal activity and avoid taxes. Mr Modi was clear in stating, 'The magnitude of cash in circulation is directly linked to the level of corruption,' in his televised address that day.

The decision was significant for it affected as much as 86 per cent of the cash then in use as India was still largely a 'cash-based' economy. For a country such as India, with many still residing in remote parts of the nation, it was certainly a period of tumult and quite a bit of chaos.

The announcement of demonetization was followed by pro-longed cash shortages in the weeks that followed, which created significant disruption throughout the economy. People seeking to exchange their banknotes and to obtain the new series had to stand in lengthy queues. There was much comment and con-jecture as to the effects of demonetization, on the economy, on whether it had succeeded in its objectives, etc.

Cut to 2019 and the same prime minister's government announced suddenly during the month of August that Article 370, a provision in the Constitution of India that provided special status to the state of Jammu & Kashmir (J&K), was being abrogated. The state was to be bifurcated into two

Union Territories, one with a legislature (Jammu & Kashmir) and one without (Ladakh).

Now let us cast our minds further back and remember the 'Father of Modern Turkey', a remarkable man called Kemal Atatürk. The Turkish leader initiated a series of reforms encompassing major political, legal, religious, cultural, social and economic policy changes that were designed to convert the new Turkish republic into a secular, modern nation-state in accordance with what came to be called the Kemalist ideology.

Central to this ideology was the integration of Turkey with Western European ideals and culture, casting behind centuries of its Islamic history. The political reforms involved a number of fundamental institutional changes that brought an end to many traditions. Reforms began with the modernization of the constitution in 1924, and the adoption of European laws in the new republic. This was followed by the doing away of all religious aspects in the administration; Tukey was to be completely secular and modern, especially its education system.

Atatürk replaced the canonical law that was in place, adopting the Swiss Civil Code and the Italian Penal Code. Remarkably, and perhaps most significantly, the reforms brought about the complete separation of government and religion. Educational institutions and the army were also separated from politics. The exclusion of religion from the nation's public life was probably the most far-reaching, for it saw many religious schools being closed down, and religion become a totally personal matter, and have nothing to do with the state. Co-educational institutes became the norm, with much emphasis on education of women and girls.

Atatürk had the charisma that few other leaders had, perhaps similar to that of John F. Kennedy in the USA. He tasked himself as a leader who would bring modernity to Turkey so that it could take its place among the leading nations of the 20th century. Atatürk's charisma was no doubt a factor that helped the Turkish people adapt to the rapid change that 'Kemalism' espoused. However, they had to adapt, almost miraculously, within a relatively short period in which the drastic changes were implemented.

Atatürk also did much to further women's rights, introducing laws that would see women enjoy rights equal to men, giving them the right to vote and to be elected to parliament. Other laws drastically reformed marriage (abolishing polygamy) and family relations (notably equal rights for women in divorce, custody, and inheritance).

Perhaps as remarkably as other reforms, Atatürk managed to 'secularize' even clothing—men were banned from wearing the Muslim cap called 'fez'; and wearing of the headscarf or veils in public buildings was also banned.

What was so notable about these people and incidents? There is one common aspect that is all important—the people behind them and the changes they brought were 'BOLD'. This chapter is not about espousing a particular political party or political ideology, but it is about espousing the need to be Bold. The incidents mentioned here are about people 'biting the bullet', attacking issues that involved significant change (and not just change, but significant disruption) and trying to make a difference.

BURNING ONE'S BOAT

There are many incidents mentioned in the history of various countries when a certain commander, having landed in a new country, ordered his men to destroy their ships, so that they could not think of going back—the only way was to go forward boldly—the commander and his men would have to conquer the country or be killed.

- Perhaps the oldest such incident refers to the Roman myth of Aeneas, who burned his boats after conquering territory in Italy.

- One more such incident was in AD 711, when commander Tariq ibn Ziyad invaded the Iberian peninsula, and reportedly ordered his men to burn their ships.

- Another such incident was in AD 1519, perhaps more well known, it is said to have been initiated by the Spanish conquistador Hernando Cortes. Cortes ordered his ships to be scuttled when they reached Mexico.

- Two similar methods are said to have been used in China during the Chu–Han contention.

- Similar incidents were recorded in other countries including Myanmar, etc.

Most of the incidents centre around the common theme which the commander wished to convey to his troops; there was NO turning back. You need to either win or perish. To an extent, Mahatma Gandhi's clear message during the Quit India Movement in Indian history in 1942 was similar. He told his men to 'Do or Die'. We shall throw the British out or die in the attempt, he said.

GOING ALL OUT

Why am I recounting these incidents and pieces from history? It is because if you are to succeed in a new initiative, even in the corporate world, one has to be bold. One cannot make half-hearted attempts, ready to backtrack and revert to the old way of doing things at the slightest sign of trouble.

Unfortunately, I have often seen that faced with important strategic choices and turning points in one's career, many executives wish to first 'test the waters'. They are not fully committed to the change or new technology that is being considered and keep the path of 'flight back to the old' open. Very often, that is the path that they end up taking, beating a hasty retreat and reverting to the old way.

How many times have people told you when you came up with an idea, 'Oh, that's already been tried?' Worse, how many times have you been told that it has been tried elsewhere, rather than in your own organization?

What are the number of times you have seen truly bold decisions being made in your corporate career? On the other hand, how many times have you been frustrated by this apparent lack of willingness to move forward with genuine commitment?

I will like to posit to those who prefer taking baby steps when faced with something new. In case you feel you will derive some of the benefits of the new product, approach or innovation while avoiding the risks or pitfalls, you are absolutely wrong.

Baby steps give you the risks but bring virtually zero benefits. Never does innovation or the 'new way' work unless you and your team are fully committed to it. You have to believe in it fully, do your research and evaluation to make sure that it is the right solution, but once you complete this, you have to implement the new way in full letter and spirit; and not just 'test the waters'.

If you try to take a step forward while keeping the path open to take two back, you are only going to end up with the two or more steps backward. For your competitor will have pushed you back even more. That is why people and companies are often told to 'change, before they have to'.

One person who was bold in his corporate career to the point of being audacious was Dr Subhas Chandra, the founder of the Essel (Zee) Group, with whom I had the fortune of working for some time. At a time when being an entrepreneur was not really fashionable, he had the guts and gumption to found many companies; and many of these were in sectors that had just opened up to the private sector. Hence, Dr Chandra founded the first private company in these areas. Examples included the first private television channel (called Zee), the first Direct-to-Home (DTH) entity and the first cable network.

Dr Chandra was always willing to take a chance, and his thinking and approach reflected it not only while commencing something new but also while running an established firm (unfortunately, his entrepreneurial spirit was not always taken forward by the people in charge of these entities).

BE READY TO 'FAIL BIG'

But there are few who exhibit such entrepreneurial thinking in established companies. They could do well to remember the words of Denzel Washington, the famous actor, made at Dillard University, Louisiana, USA in 2015.

> Fail big, that's right. Fail big, today is the beginning of the rest of your life and you can be just – be very frightening. And it's a new world out there, it's a mean world out there. You only live once, so do what you feel passionate about, passionate about. Take chances professionally, don't be afraid to fail, there is an old IQ test [that] was nine dots and you had to

draw five lines with the pencil within the nine dots without lifting the pencil.

The only way to do it was to go outside the box. So don't be afraid to go outside the box. Don't be afraid to think outside the box. Don't be afraid to fail big, to dream big, but remember, dreams without goals, are just dreams.

Fail big? Is that really sensible advice? I have often thought about it. I think Denzel Washington got it right. You have to be willing to think outside the box and tread new paths and be a trail for others to perhaps follow- you be the trailblazer, let others take it up from where you left off.

If one indeed wishes to blaze a trail and go to areas where others haven't been, once again the mindset is very import- ant. And that mindset is one of being ready for failure. For if you are only doing things where success is guaran- teed, you aren't really leaving a trail or doing something that is truly remarkable. You are only following tried and tested techniques, walking down paths where many have walked before.

Those who wish to make a difference therefore, must be ready to fail; and fail big. Denzel Washington ended the same speech with exactly the same thoughts:

'Don't just aspire to make a living. Aspire to make a difference. Thank you.' And for making a difference, one has to be bold.

'NEVER, NEVER, NEVER GIVE UP'

But being bold and ready to fail if need be is a necessary condition towards achieving success, not a sufficient one. The sufficient condition that accompanies this is having what is called Tenacity.

In the previous section, I recounted Denzel Washington's speech at a University in the United States. Let us complement that speech with this famous incident involving Winston Churchill.

The British bulldog as he has been termed, the man famous for his 'Blood, toil, tears and Sweat' speech was invited to speak to the boys of the famous British school, Harrow, near London. Churchill had in fact attended the same school himself when he was young.

Popular history has it that on being invited to speak, Churchill went to the podium and said in a stentorian voice the famous words: 'Never give up. Never give up.' And one final time loudly, 'Never, never give up,' and then sat down. His address was over.[1]

The famous American football coach, Vincent Thomas 'Vince' Lombardi is also credited with having said something on similar lines: 'Winners never quit; and quitters never win.'

Tenacity is indeed most important. It is the critical aspect that separates those who succeed from those who fall by the wayside. Indeed, it makes those who have it appear to have special qualities.

Einstein, recognized this, stating, that the world only saw his final success and called him a genius; while ignoring the thousands of times he had tried and failed. He is credited with saying 'It's not that I'm so smart, I just stay with problems longer.'

This is a very important aspect in overcoming any obstacle, especially in a corporate setting. You have to keep turning the problem over in your mind; and take responsibility towards

---

[1] In reality, Churchill's speech was a bit longer, but this is how it is recounted by most—as one of the most pithy and concise speeches ever, conveying its meaning very effectively.

resolving it. While you may take a break or two from thinking over it, don't give up on it; keep returning to the matter till you resolve it.

This tenacity is the source of innovation, for if you keep thinking about the issue, sooner or later, your mind will start looking at it from new perspectives or try to find alternatives. But if you don't stick with it, the mind will not have the opportunity to come up with something new.

I often give the following simple case to my students or those I interview for executive roles. It goes like this:

> You are in charge of a factory. You are planning to increase production at this factory and need a higher electricity load. You apply for this increase, but find that the local linesman wants a bribe for getting things done. He does not necessarily explicitly ask for one, but points to any number of technical constraints which prevent the additional load from being sanctioned and connected. You understand that this linesman is going to delay your sanction unless you pay up.
>
> What are you going to do?

I generally tell students to write down their thoughts. When I look at their sheets, there are invariably three types of submissions:

- Those who say it is best to pay off the linesman given the small amount in question and the fact that this is a common problem in India and often resolved in a similar manner: 'everyone does it'

- A few who say they will not pay even if it means not getting the work done

- Those who explore alternatives to paying off the linesman

I then tell my students to re-work their thoughts using a decision tree and consider the alternative possibilities. For example, one way forward could be to approach the superior of this linesman towards getting the work done. But what if he also doesn't agree? Then what is the next possible solution?

In relatively simplistic terms, one can represent the alternative solutions in the following categories (such an approach is beneficial for you can see that it applies in general terms to other problems as well, this case being only an example):

- Solutions that centre around bypassing the need for additional electricity or finding alternatives to getting the additional electricity without being dependent on the linesman. This includes:
  - Reworking the additional load requirement or optimizing it by say reducing the load elsewhere or working in shifts, etc.
  - Using alternative power sources such as a captive power generation unit running on diesel
  - Using solar power panels, etc.
- Solutions that centre around bypassing the particular troublesome linesman. These include:
  - Going to his superior
  - Bringing the matter to the attention of senior functionaries in the government. You can write to the local MP or even the chief minister, for example.

The case is so structured that whatever the solution proposed, I come up with some objection or the other to say it 'can't be done'. Given the solutions mentioned earlier, the students may be told that working in shifts is not possible, the MP ignores your mail, the superior asks for an even bigger bribe(!), etc.

The case is actually one that tests tenacity (along with ethics). How many possible solutions can you think of when you are told that your thoughts won't work? The faculty administering such a case will keep telling you that, thereby testing you.

Will you keep trying, keep plugging away; and coming up with more and more potentialities? Or would you say quickly, 'Let me give the bribe and be done with it.' Think of these possibilities closely. Is there a bit of 'intellectual laziness' influencing your choice? Are you really looking at all possibilities?

I often use this case or similar ones during job interviews or for selecting students for an MBA course. The way they approach the matter provides a good insight into their thought process and perhaps even their character.

Many are quick to suggest paying off the person; and a few stick to their ideals, refusing to bribe. There are however, a few who keep suggesting various possibilities and evaluating them. When we find someone who does this, we know we have a winner, for they never quit.

ANNEXURE: THE 9 DOT PUZZLE

This chapter refers to the famous 9 dot puzzle (Denzel Washington had mentioned it in his speech.) What is it?

This is one of the most well-known illustrations of the concept of 'thinking out of the box'. This is how the puzzle goes.

Following are nine dots arranged in a set of three square rows. You have to connect all the dots, by using four straight lines only which must go through the middle of each and every dot without taking the pencil off the paper. Try it out; and do not give up till you have solved it:

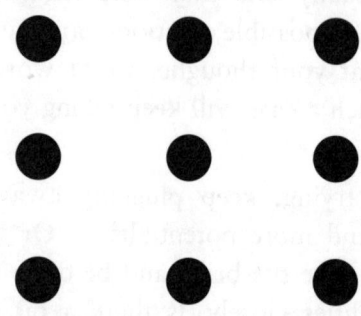

Solution to the 9-dot puzzle

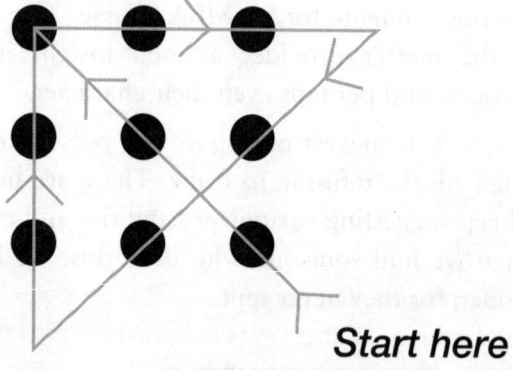

Start here

Now think about how you went about solving the puzzle. Did you try out various possibilities using the 'trial and error' approach or did you come up with a strategy? Take a couple of minutes thinking about how you went about it and what changes in your thoughts you needed along your way.

The beauty of this puzzle is that in this case, you literally have to 'think out of the box' to solve the puzzle. Your pen or pencil must go outside the box of the dots to be able to solve it. Almost all of us would have started by trying to draw all the lines within the dots. That does not get us anywhere. Yet we will initially persist with keeping the lines inside the 'box'. Why?

- Perhaps we stick to the box because there is nothing outside the set of dots to associate to.

- We assume we are constrained by the 'boundary' of the dots. Even though it is purely imaginary; there was no specification of such a boundary. We only have assumed that the boundary exists.

- We assume we will eventually get there so we keep *trying the same way* but harder.

So what does the puzzle teach us?

- See what is allowed explicitly and what is not. But when faced with a problem, do not make implicit assumptions that certain things are not allowed. Ask and clarify whether self-imposed boundaries are indeed to be imposed.

- Constrained by perceptions? Very often, our way of looking at problems is constrained by our own perceptions. You may need to break out of these perceptions to arrive at a solution.

- Wrong problem definition? If the way we define the issue or problem is faulty, no number of attempts or hard work will solve the real problem. We have to re-define the problem from scratch.

- Always investigate the boundaries. Try and understand carefully what are the boundaries which the solution must fit into. Are these boundaries based on your own perceptions or reality? What are the possibilities if you push the boundaries?

- Don't always think hard work is the solution. When I was younger, I used to say whenever I could not do anything that I would just put my head down and work harder. Yet gradually I realized that this does not always work. If the process is wrong, or the problem definition is faulty, we cannot succeed just be trying harder. We have to approach it with a different mindset, not with more physical effort.

Chapter 14

Culture Eats Strategy for Breakfast

The best time to make up your mind about people is never.
—Katharine Hepburn in The Philadelphia Story

Peter F. Drucker, the 'father of modern management', according to many, once made a telling statement, 'Culture eats strategy for breakfast'. Not everyone can grasp the importance of what he meant the first time he/she comes across this quote, but for someone who has worked in corporate roles, his statement rings so very true.

All the time spent on planning, ideating and strategizing comes to naught if the culture of the organization does not support the plans and strategies that have been made. A traditionally bureaucratic company may make plans envisaging quicker response to customer needs, but its culture gets in the way of realizing its strategic plans.

A company traditionally focused on a particular industry may wish to enter another, but its culture is not attuned to this diversification move. For 'this is how things have always been done here'; and the new industry requires things to be done differently.

In addition, many organizations take fresh MBAs and put them into strategy roles to inject 'fresh blood' or 'new ideas'. But these youngsters soon come up against a big wall, that of the organization culture. This often is insurmountable, leading to much angst, heartburn and frustration.

I experienced a lot of this first hand, when I was fresh into the corporate world. I was called a 'loose cannon' more than once and there were many tough learnings for me. Nowadays, when someone makes this sort of a comment, I take it as a compliment, for it makes me happy that I still retain some of the fire that I originally had; and in fact, when I moved on from the Vedanta Group, I mentioned in my parting e-mail to my colleagues that my greatest achievement was that after seven years, I was leaving with the same pride and enthusiasm that I had when I joined the firm in my late 20s.

But here are some of the key learnings:

First, I learnt that often your boss does not want you to do what is best for the company. He wants you to do what shows him/her in the best light. Sometimes, only the promoter really cares about the company; many other people, however high up they are, are wary of anything that challenges their own position (and hence which upsets the status quo). So beware when proposing new technologies—it may make your boss redundant for a new set or skills are required at the top.

Second, I learnt that often it does not matter what you suggest; it matters on whose shoulders you are appearing to stand on when you make the suggestions. In a particular Indian conglomerate, I was working as part of the chairman's office in a senior role. I discovered that when it was apparent that the suggestions were mine, I was often ignored; when I said the same thing without making it explicit whether the suggestion was mine or coming from the group chairman, the suggestion was treated as if it was manna from heaven!

Third, people often look at aspects like to whom you are connected with, whose ears you have, whose doors are open to you. Very often, this overshadows all else. This manifests itself in much chat about everything about a person apart from work, his/her qualifications, his/her spouse's job, his/ her background, etc. The way these matters are probed is itself an art; for the questions are never forthright, but information is pried out in clever ways.

As you can see, some of these learnings may appear cynical. I decided that rather than give way to cynicism, one must look at the funny side of it all, for what goes on behind the curtains in corporates is nothing but a soap opera and family entertainer.

With that in mind, my wife and I penned a satirical story; I would like to reproduce it here as a reflection of the realities of the corporate world and something that all of us have had to navigate through in some way or the other.

Many of you would have experienced some of the situations that the characters in this story reflect, I hope this provides some relief, while at the same time serving to bring out that the culture of the organization and that of people in general are always paramount!

This story is intended as a humorous satire; all characters are purely fictional, I would like to thank my wife Surabhi Shukla for major contributions towards this story.

'Why is there so much rush on Delhi streets even on Sunday afternoons? Where is the traffic situation heading to? Guess I am late already!' I muttered to myself as the traffic light turned red forcing me to stop just before I could turn left into Sarvapriya Vihar, a residential colony in New Delhi.

'Relax, no need to rush, you are only going for a tete-a-tete with friends, not for a corporate meeting,' I reminded myself, 'and besides, this is not just an ordinary meeting, this is THE meet, the much awaited month-end get-together for us six ladies to interact and talk about most things under the sun, express our opinions, discuss problems and share our experiences; something that keeps us rejuvenated and going for a full month. Relax? I could not in that sea of chaotic traffic which took me full one and a half hours to reach Sarvapriya Vihar from Green Park, a distance of mere 5km.

Finally, reaching the venue, I saw the group had already warmed into conversation.

Radhika, the corporate honcho, was speaking. The recent success of the Indian telecom company she worked in, especially in acquisitions abroad, which was part of her portfolio as acquisitions manager, had spurred her professional success quite well, enabling her to buy a plush flat in Gurgaon, the new so-called 'Millennium City' of National Capital Region. Never mind if the city seemed to lack in basic infrastructure.

Opening her round black eyes as wide as possible, she continued, 'My neighbour along with her regular work (which actually comprises nothing except constantly following her maid with her hand on her hip, constantly pointing out omissions to the poor creature) seems to be heading a top-notch spying agency. She has to keep records of who's who, where, how, why for every resident, visitor, trespasser maybe even stray dogs in the colony. The society security guards should take some tips from her on active vigilance!'

'Yes,' I continued, 'This is so familiar to each one of us, Indians are plagued by their curiosity to know "all" about the next person, be it an accidental co-passenger on the metro, the new next door neighbour, or a new colleague in office, within the first few minutes of interaction we need to know all the details. There is not much variety in the questions asked...begins with what are your qualifications, current job, past job, salary, and proceeds on to "family life"—married or unmarried, if still unmarried—why so, if married then how many kids, if no kids then why so, your spouse's job, salary, qualifications, own house or rented house, how much is the rent/cost of the house and so forth. The only variety one can possibly find is in the manner of interrogation: while a new bride is grilled demand-ingly, a new neighbour is questioned under the friendly "know thy neighbour" pretext; similarly, a co-passenger is spoken to in "casual time pass" terms and a new colleague interrogated discretely under "team-interaction spirit".'

'I know, I know,' quipped Amrita, 'this is a problem in most places in India, especially in Delhi, people rip your private life apart with questions under the pretext of "friendliness" and you know the worst part, despite these questions, they tend to form their own opinions and gossip about you behind your back with others.'

'Yes, I agree,' said I. 'This is the standard pattern in people, try to ascertain people's lives and if unable to do so fully, gossip and spread rumour about him/her, usually this is the case—though there may be some exceptions like Ms Udhampreet Kaur.'

'*Udhampreet Kaur?*' Chorused all five. 'Tell us more...do tell us more about her!'

'Well...,' I continued. 'Do you remember the last organization I was working in? The world's second largest publishing firm: Bucephalous Publications Ltd? Well, I was based in their head office in India—Gurgaon and that was where I got acquainted with Ms Chamanpreet Kaur.'

'Chamanpreet Kaur?' chirped in Garima, with the impatience of the youth, 'but did you not say Udhampreet Kaur earlier?'

'Hold on...hold on...she is still speaking,' said Rupali, the natural referee after years of monitoring school kids.

'Yes,' I said. 'Chamanpreet Kaur was a new joinee herself in the organization. Within a few weeks of her joining Bucephalous Publications, she managed to create so much of discord with almost everybody in the organization that soon she was referred to as "Udhampreet" meaning "discord loving" instead of "Chamanpreet" her actual name meaning "peace loving." '

'Despite this, I always felt that we submissive "workers" secretly admired her brazen attitude. Her manager, Heema, was based in Mumbai while she was based in Gurgaon. Nevertheless, she managed to exhibit her full control and terror over employees in Gurgaon through constant phone calls. People had no option but to give in to her whims and fancies, the most favourite whim of hers was the demand that people stay back in office after office hours, irrespective of whether it was required or not.

'Once Heema during Chamanpreet's initial days in office put forth her favourite demand, just as Chamanpreet had logged off for the day. While most people in her scenario would have agreed on the face of it and cribbed later amongst friends or the smarter ones would have only pretended to work late and tried to fool the outstation boss, Udhampreet was not one to go by the usual rules. She would not stoop to any such level. Her loud booming voice was heard resonating through the entire floor, categorically stating that extra work hours had not been stated in her job description or joining papers nor had been communicated to her verbally prior to her joining, hence it could not be done. I feel certain that despite the pretence of being too busy with our own work to notice, quite a few of us rejoiced internally at the conversation.'

'Yes, I agree,' said Radhika 'It must have been music to every one's ears (Heema, of course, excluded!). I wish I had the courage to tell my boss the same. He comes in casually two hours after office begins every day so obviously leaves later, but expects me to come on time and leave only after he leaves. He deliberately delays his approvals and other stuff where we have to work together, leaving me with no choice, but to stay back.

'Once in a while, if I leave when he leaves (which is, by the way, two hours after regular office timings) he makes it a point to mention how young people like me should work hard to build their career in their early lives and how at my age he used to sit in office till 10 p.m.! Such expectations should be nipped in the bud. I fully support your Chamanpreet alias Udhampreet.'

'That is not all,' said I, 'if some "senior" colleague tried to "guide" her in the work, she would tell them to push off in no uncertain terms.'

'If the cafeteria was fully occupied, Udhampreet would audibly demarcate the "culprit" eating most leisurely despite the people in queue. If that did not work she would then stand right in front of the culprit's table, glaring at him/her till he/she wrapped up fast under the obvious pressure!'

'When "snobs" sneered behind her back, cracking jokes about her green hair band and green hair clips set on her L'Oreal auburn hair to match with her green Patiala salwar kameez, she would turn around and openly question them about their smiles, freezing them in shock!'

'Quite a character!' Piped in Amrita.

'Yes, we agree!' Chorused the others.

'So,' I continued, 'for obvious reasons, Chamanpreet was soon popularly known as Udhampreet. Now we add another character to the story—enter Ms Arundhati Sen, the new picture perfect employee in Bucephalous Publications Ltd. Alighting from her Honda CRV, in exclusive Ritu Kumar creations, she turned heads instantly. She did not exactly "fit" the criteria of a typical content developer in the industry— the middle-class worker who slogs long hours for a pittance. Money definitely did not seem to be the motivation behind her working in her current profile. Unlike most others, she seemed to actually enjoy her work, was willing to work late, come to office on weekends and go the extra mile, which naturally won her boss's appreciation. Soft spoken yet dignified, confident and professional in her dealings and conversation, she was the "hot" topic of discussion for one and all behind her back.

'Discreet and not so discreet questions about her family background did not reveal much; her husband worked in a consulting firm and was responsible for getting business for the company, the couple had two children and they lived in Gurgaon was all people could elicit out of her.'

'Cafeteria gossips usually ran like this: "Why is she (with Honda CRV) working here for the peanuts that they give content developers?," asked Mrs A. "Well, how do you know that she is being given the same pittance as others?," questioned Mrs B. "Because that is the average industry payment standard, you know that!" "Yes, but is she average? Look at her diamonds, sarees, sandals, cars! Is she average? Can all this come from this work or from her *agent* husband?" quipped Mrs B again. "How do you know that her husband is an agent?" questioned some knowledge seeker. "Obvious," came the answer. "Did she not say that her husband has to get business for the company? Such jobs are done by agents, I know all about corporates. Besides, don't you see her overenthusiasm at work, comes on time, works late, is in office on weekends and the kind of smile the Boss gives her? Does it all not point at something?" "Oh!" echoed all. There were several such gossipy stories doing rounds, but almost nobody had the face to ask her directly, *almost* that is!'

'One day Arundhati was sipping tea alone in the cafeteria when Udhampreet passing by, decided to join her. This was the first time that the two were having a direct face-to-face interaction. Udhampreet after the customary introduction of names and profiles shot out questions at her straight out of a quiver.

"What are your qualifications?"

"MSc. Microbiology"

"MSc! Have you done PhD as well?"

"Well, I was doing it, but had to leave it half way due to personal reasons, nevertheless, my love for the subject remains. This job involves so much reading and research that I feel my PhD days are back," she answered with a nostalgic smile.

"Where do you live?"

"The Millennium condominiums, Gurgaon."

"Condominium? How many rooms does it have?"

"It has...err... It has two floors."

"Two floors!! It is on rent or your own house?"

"No, not on rent."

"It must have been bought on huge loans then, the EMIs should be massive then! Which school do your kids go to?"

"The Scholars International."

"How much is the monthly fee per child?"

"Hmm...about 40,000."

"40k! That's 80k for 2 kids per month! What do they charge such a huge fee for?"'

'By now the crowd in the cafeteria had swollen yet there was pin drop silence. Craning necks were visible everywhere. People were aghast with surprise, but the questions kept firing.

"80k per month for school fees, luxury condominium, what does your husband do?"

"Hmmm...he works in BCP, a consulting firm."

"What does he do?"

"Well, he is...well...he gets business for the company."'

'By now some onlookers had turned red in the face; others were looking at each other whispering how uncouth, unprofessional Udhampreet was and how she was an embarrassment to other professionals around.

"Oh…like an agent you mean…that is not so good. If tomorrow you lose your job will your husband be able to pay the fees of the kids and the EMIs? Have you thought of that?"'

'This question caused pin drop silence. Several jaws dropped. All eyes turned to Arundhati to see her reaction. Udhampreet on her part looked normal. Arundhati looked aghast but sat in silence for a while. And then to everybody's surprise, she started laughing heartily. "I hope so, my dear friend, I do hope Arvind manages to run the household, without my job," she said in an amused manner.'

'"Is your husband that Arvind? Arvind Sen, the Global CEO of BCP?" Asked someone hesitantly, almost in a half-whisper.

"Yes," she smiled. "It happens to be the same Arvind. I appreciate your frankness, my friend," she continued conversing with Udhampreet. "Unlike most others, you had the forthrightness to be open about your curiosity and not presume things."'

'"I prefer straightforward people," was her last sentence as she left the cafeteria, away from the new crowd which came forward to befriend her; the wife of one of the most well-known CEOs in the country.'

What does this story bring out? I have used it as an illustration of how some organizations have a strong 'grapevine' and the dangers of over-indulging rumours and speculations. This aspect is often seen when things appear to go wrong; and there are much whispers floating in the corridors. What is best in such a situation? Perhaps it is best to go and openly ask about what is happening, rather than indulge in idle gossip.

That is from the employee's perspective. From the perspective of the management, when one is framing strategy, especially those involving radical shifts, open and honest communication of the new direction that the company may be taking or may need to take due to external circumstances is very important. This can be done through a forum such as a 'town hall' discussion or other such ways.

In the absence of adequate communication, you can only expect the grapevine to get active and the organization to represent a fish market where rumours float around. Over a period of time, this demotivates people, for they feel left out and clueless as to what is actually taking place. It also leads to issues of stress and burnout.

EPILOGUE

There was once a person who received the following e-mail at office:

'Management has noted your suggestion regarding the usage of new technology X. However, after due consideration and evaluation of the pros and cons, the management has decided to go ahead with using the existing product and technology.

We thank you for your valuable suggestion.'

The person who received the e-mail starts writing his reply:

'How can management make such a decision? The new technology has proven itself far better in all tests. It appears rather foolish to ignore emerging trends and technologies and putting one's faith rather in what is obsolete. This decision will set us back by at least a few years, and....'

Having written this, he suddenly seems to realize that perhaps his reply is too strongly worded. So he deletes his entire mail and commences writing a new email thus:

'I appreciate management having made this decision. However, I would like to point out that I strongly advocate revisiting the decision. I personally feel that the new technology could help us leap-frog over our competitors, helping us....'

The person again stops writing. He pauses, thinks again, deletes the e-mail and starts again:

'I appreciate the judgement and wisdom of our management. However, could I get the opportunity to present my case....'

For the third time, he stops and deletes the e-mail.

Finally, he writes the following:

'Ok,' and presses the Send button.

This is one of my favourite stories pertaining to corporate life. There is so much that this story tells us!

As corporate leaders, we must realize what our people really feel and as corporate workers we must be able to express what we feel and think without the fear of consequences. In this example, there was so much left unsaid, there was so much angst, passion and feeling that preceded the 'ok'. Are we really in touch with what our people feel? Do we understand their motivations and passion? Do we understand what is behind the seeming assent? Is it genuine support or is merely hierarchy masking people's feelings and emotions?

On the other hand, if we are not leaders yet, the story teaches us much. It is very important in corporate life, to be able to 'express oneself'. Most employees curb their natural instincts, passions, motivations and fire to what they feel the company demands. But it is important to find the space to express oneself, especially what motivates or excites you with regard to work.

The best companies and the best leaders succeed in offering this space to individuals. Be it companies such as 3M or Google, the ones that are the most innovative, that create the most value are the ones that offer this space to individuals, giving them time to pursue their areas of passion.

Leaders also understand that the most productive employees are the ones that don't have to deal with the frustrations of ideas that are blocked from seeing the light of day. They allow people to express themselves, not through their words, but through their work.

Mahatma Gandhi had once said, 'Happiness is when What you think, What you feel and What you Do are in Harmony.' The best leaders provide for this.

ABOUT THE AUTHOR

Sidharth Balakrishna holds an MBA from the Indian Institute of Management (IIM) Calcutta and an Economics degree from the Shri Ram College of Commerce (SRCC), Delhi University. He has over 15 years of experience in the media and entertainment, artificial intelligence, energy, infrastructure and education sectors.

He has been an executive (whole time), Board Director and Chief Strategy and Innovation Officer at the Essel (Zee) Group, and is leading several strategic initiatives in digital transformation and artificial intelligence. He has led strategy and headed many large projects in the fields of oil & gas, renewable energy, education and water. Sidharth Balakrishna has also been a strategy consultant with Accenture and KPMG. Some of the projects that he has led have been awarded nationally and internationally.

He is a mentor to start-ups with MIT, Boston, USA, as well as MassChallenge Boston and Tel Aviv, Israel.

Mr Balakrishna has also written five books. He is a visiting faculty at a number of management institutes in India and delivers full credit courses at IIM Indore on artificial intelligence and strategy at FMS, Delhi University.

He has presented at a number of international fora, in more than 10 countries, including London, Amsterdam, Muscat, Dubai, Myanmar, Mozambique, Kuwait, New Delhi, Goa and Mumbai. He has been a columnist with the *Economic Times*, the London School of Economics, and has written several articles. Sidharth has been interviewed by the media a number of times and was featured in 2018 on the cover of the *Corporate Citizen* magazine. A chapter was dedicated to him in the book *Heroes amongst Us* recently and the Delhi University awarded him for his work in the media sector in 2019.